ZONDERkidz

ZONDERKIDZ

The Beginner's Bible Preschool Math Workbook
Copyright © 2022 by Zondervan
Illustrations © 2022 by Zondervan

Requests for information should be addressed to:
Zonderkidz, 3900 *Sparks Dr. SE, Grand Rapids, Michigan 49546*

ISBN: 978-0-310-13895-2

Illustrations: Denis Alonso
Design: Diane Mielke

Printed in the United States

22 23 24 25 /CWM/ 6 5 4 3 2 1

Table of Contents

Practicing Number 1

Trace and write number 1.

Practicing Number 1

Trace and write the word one.

one   one

one

one

Practicing Number 2

Trace and write number 2.

2 2 2 2 2 2

2

2

Practicing Number 2

Trace and write the word two.

two two

two

two

Practicing Number 3

Trace and write number 3.

3 3 3 3 3 3

3

3

Practicing Number 3

Trace and write the word three.

three three

three

three

Practicing Number 4

Trace and write number 4.

4 4 4 4 4 4

4

4

Practicing Number 4

Trace and write the word four.

Practicing Number 5

Trace and write number 5.

5 5 5 5 5 5

5

5

Practicing Number 5

Trace and write the word five.

Practicing Number 6

Trace and write number 6.

Practicing Number 6

Trace and write the word six.

Practicing Number 7

Trace and write number 7.

7 7 7 7 7 7

7

7

Practicing Number 7

Trace and write the word seven.

seven seven

seven

seven

Practicing Number 8

Trace and write number 8.

8 8 8 8 8 8

Practicing Number 8

Trace and write the word eight.

Practicing Number 9

Trace and write number 9.

9 9 9 9 9 9 9

Practicing Number 9

Trace and write the word nine.

nine nine

nine

nine

Practicing Number 10

Trace and write number 10.

Practicing Number 10

Trace and write the word ten.

ten ten

ten

ten

Practicing Number 11

Trace and write number 11.

Practicing Number 11

Trace and write the word eleven.

eleven eleven

eleven

eleven

Practicing Number 12

Trace and write number 12.

Practicing Number 12

Trace and write the word twelve.

twelve twelve

twelve

twelve

Practice 13 and Thirteen

Trace and write the number and the word.

Practice 14 and Fourteen

Trace and write the number and the word.

Practice 15 and Fifteen

Trace and write the number and the word.

★ Practice ★ 15 ★ and ★ Fifteen ★

Practice 16 and Sixteen

Trace and write the number and the word.

Practice 17 and Seventeen

Trace and write the number and the word.

Practice 18 and Eighteen

Trace and write the number and the word.

Practice 19 and Nineteen

Trace and write the number and the word.

19 19 19

19 19 19

19 19 19

nineteen

nineteen

nineteen

nineteen

Practice 19 and Nineteen

Practice 20 and Twenty

Trace and write the number and the word.

We Can Count

Count. Circle the matching number for each.

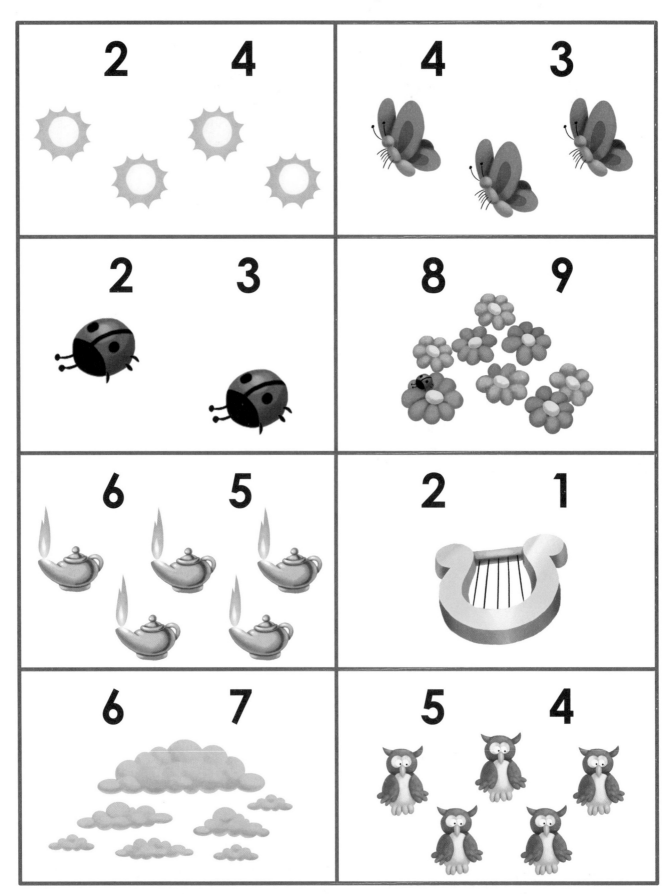

Let's Count

Count. Circle the matching number for each.

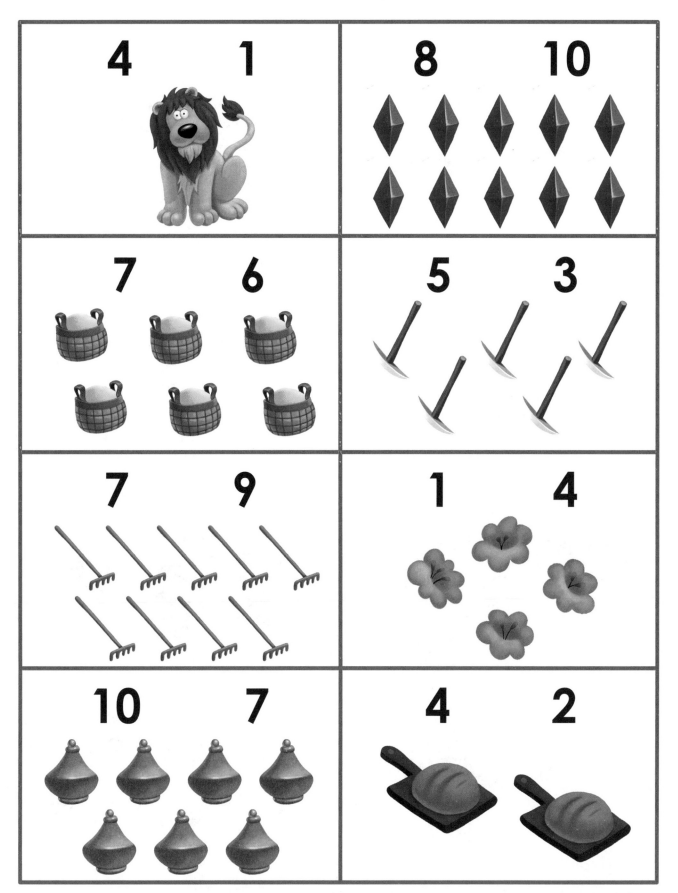

Counting Blessings

Count. Circle the matching number for each.

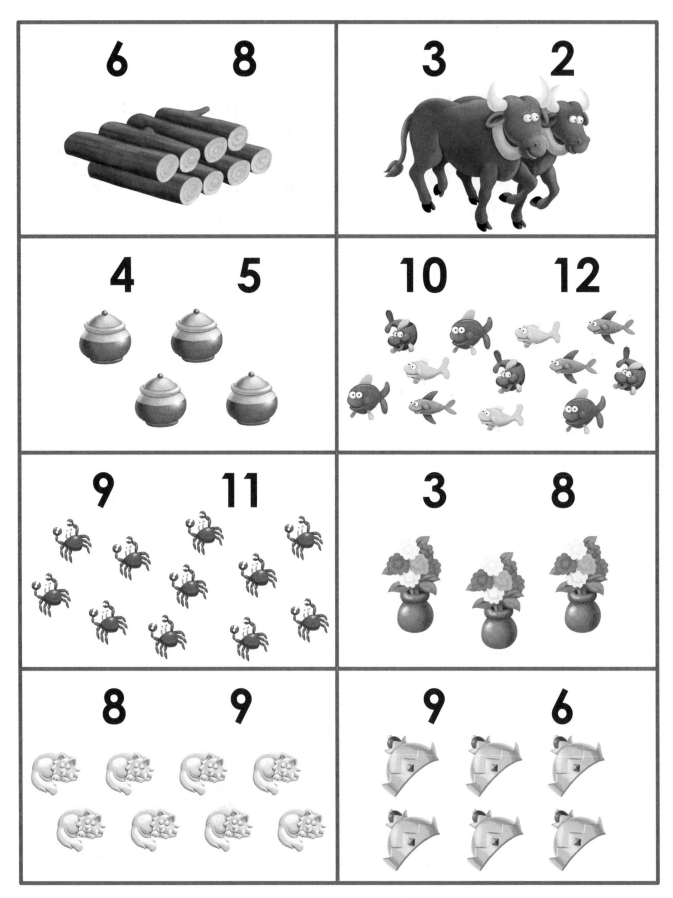

Count Down

Count. Circle the matching number for each.

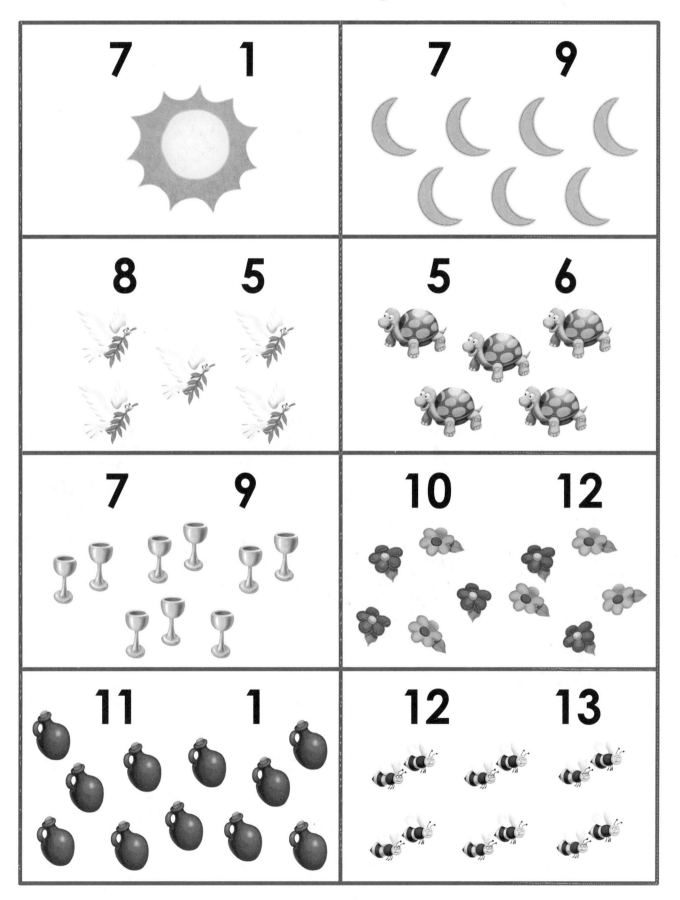

Match It!

Draw a line from each number to the matching set of items.

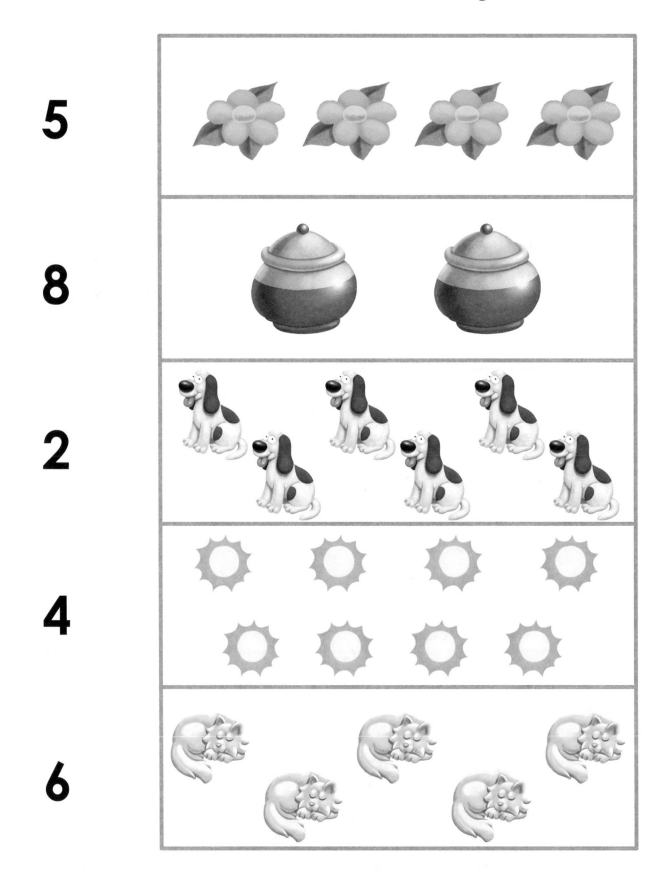

5

8

2

4

6

Match It Up

Draw a line from each number to the matching set of items.

10

1

3

7

12

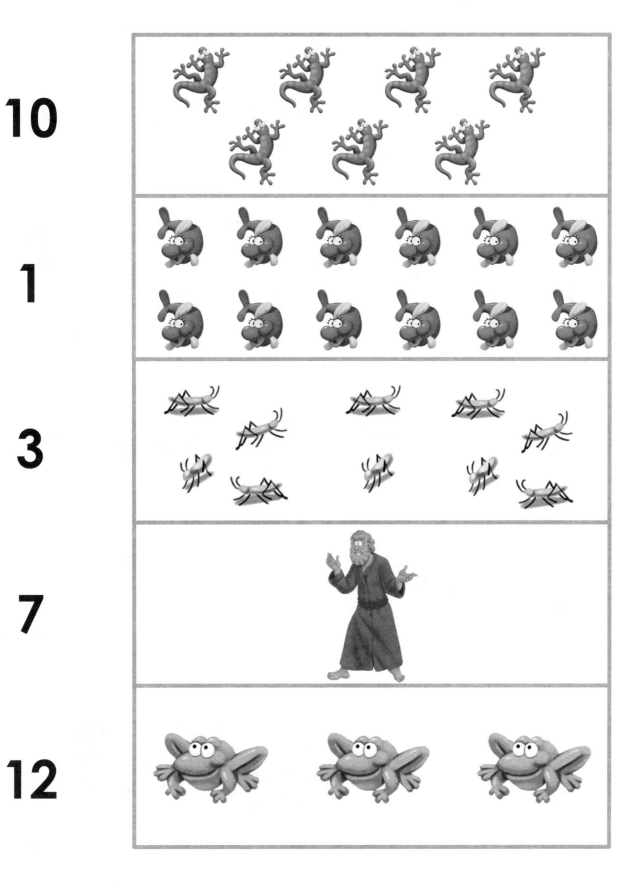

Match Game

Draw a line from each number to the matching set of items.

9

11

4

6

8

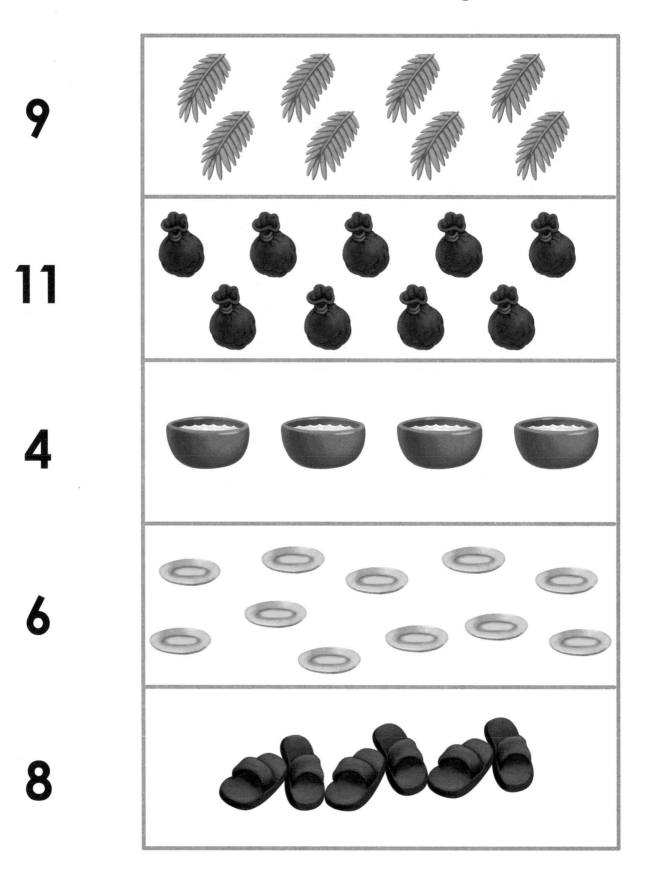

It's a Match

Draw a line from each number to the matching set of items.

1

5

7

10

2

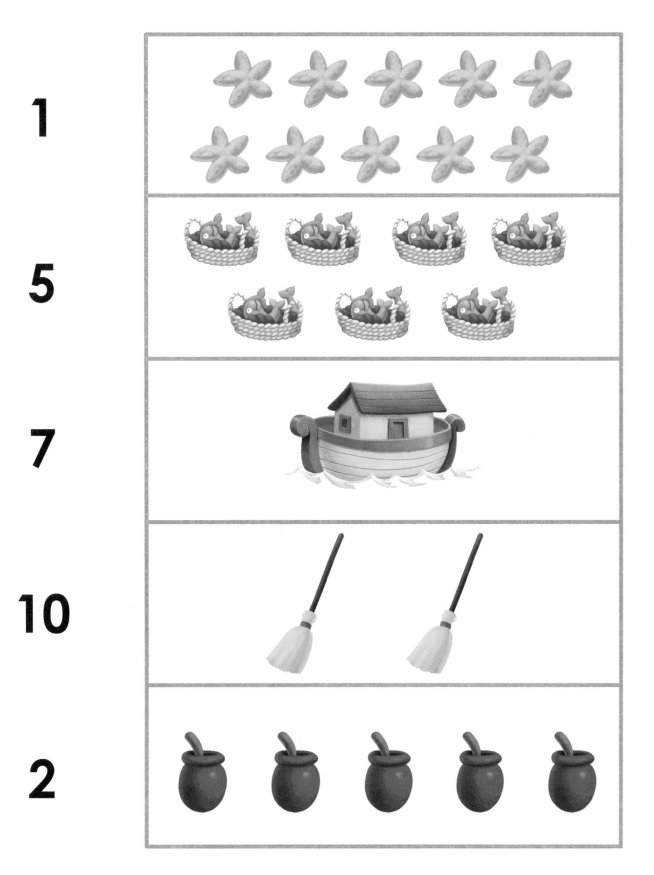

Number Match

Match the number with the number word. Draw a line.

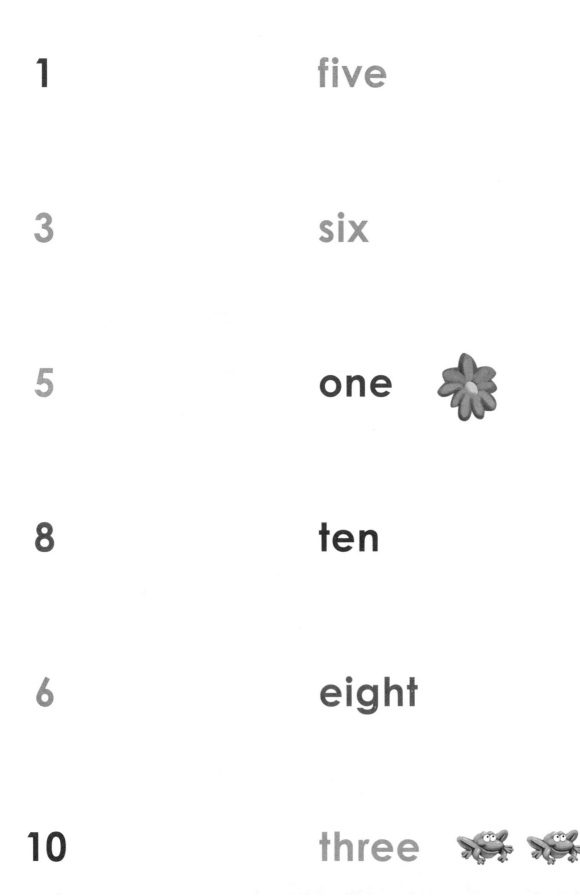

1   five

3   six

5   one

8   ten

6   eight

10   three

Number Match Again

Match the number with the number word. Draw a line.

7   eleven

9   two

2   twelve

4   seven

11   four

12   nine

Never Forget

God will never forget us. He loves us.
Fill in the blank with the missing number.

3 ___ 5 6 7

1 2 3 ___ 5

6 7 ___ 9 10

___ 5 6 7 8

8 9 10 ___ 12

2 3 4 5 ___

What Is Missing?

Fill in the blanks with the missing numbers.

___   ___   **3**   **4**   **5**

3   ___   ___   6   7

6   7   8   ___   ___

5   ___   7   8   ___

8   ___   **10**   ___   **12**

Raindrop Numbers

The rain stopped and
Noah saw a rainbow!
Fill in the missing numbers.

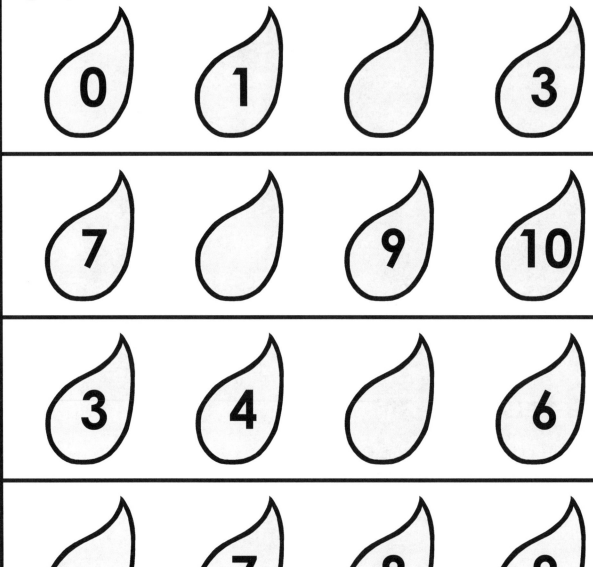

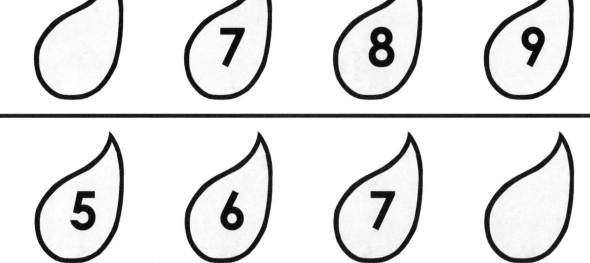

Fill the Jars

Fill in the jars with the missing numbers.

Draw and Count

Draw and color the correct number of God's creations.

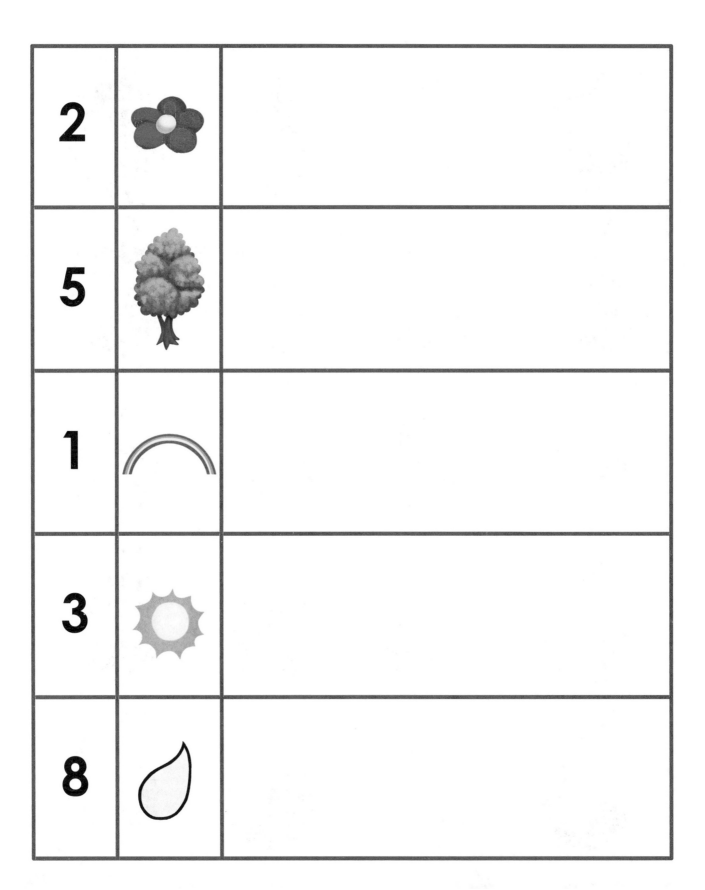

2	(flower)	
5	(tree)	
1	(rainbow)	
3	(sun)	
8	(raindrop)	

Draw It

Draw and color the correct number.

Count to 10

Fill in the missing numbers. Say "NO!" to the sneaky snake when you fill in each row.

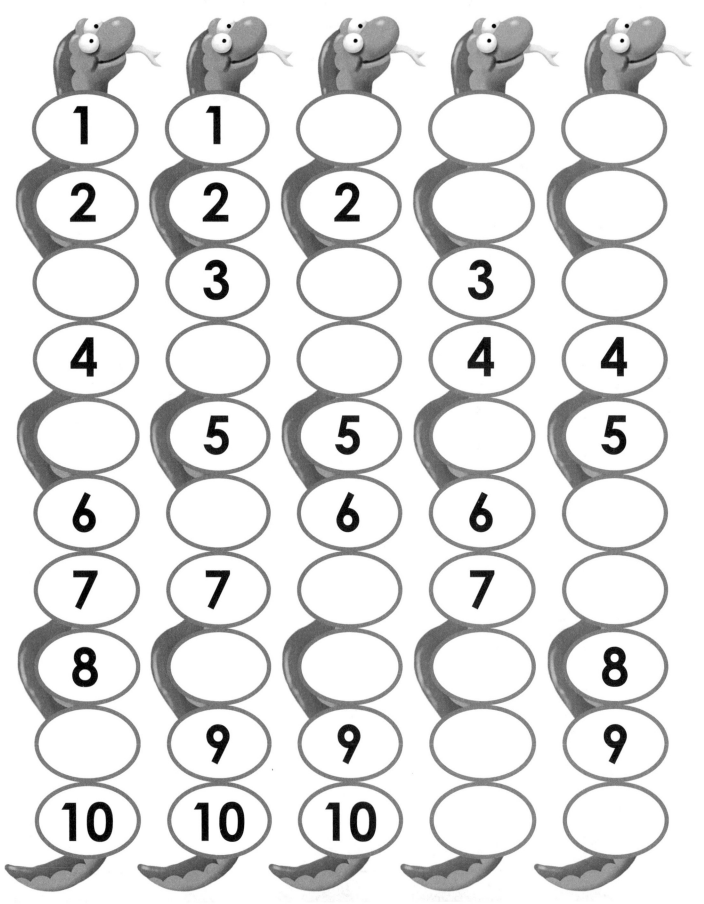

Do It Again

Fill in the missing numbers. Say "I love God!" when you fill in each row.

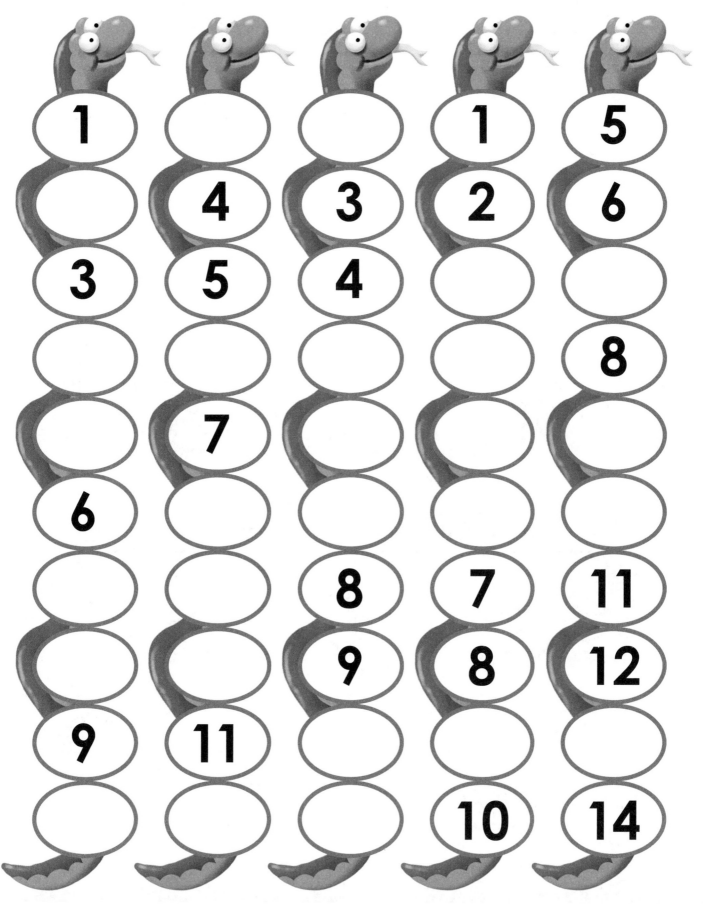

Row 1: 1, _, 3, _, _, 6, _, _, 9, _

Row 2: _, 4, 5, _, 7, _, _, _, 11, _

Row 3: _, 3, 4, _, _, _, 8, 9, _, _

Row 4: 1, 2, _, _, _, _, 7, 8, _, 10

Row 5: 5, 6, _, 8, _, _, 11, 12, _, 14

All Together

Look at these things God made. Count them. Write
how many. Then write how many all together.

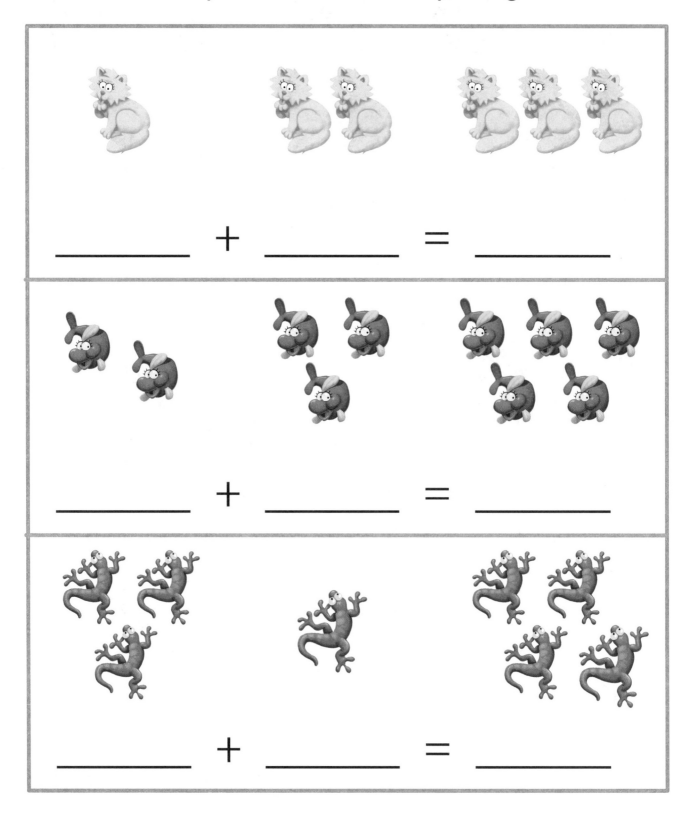

_____ + _____ = _____

_____ + _____ = _____

_____ + _____ = _____

All Together Again

Look at these things God made. Count them. Write
how many. Then write how many all together.

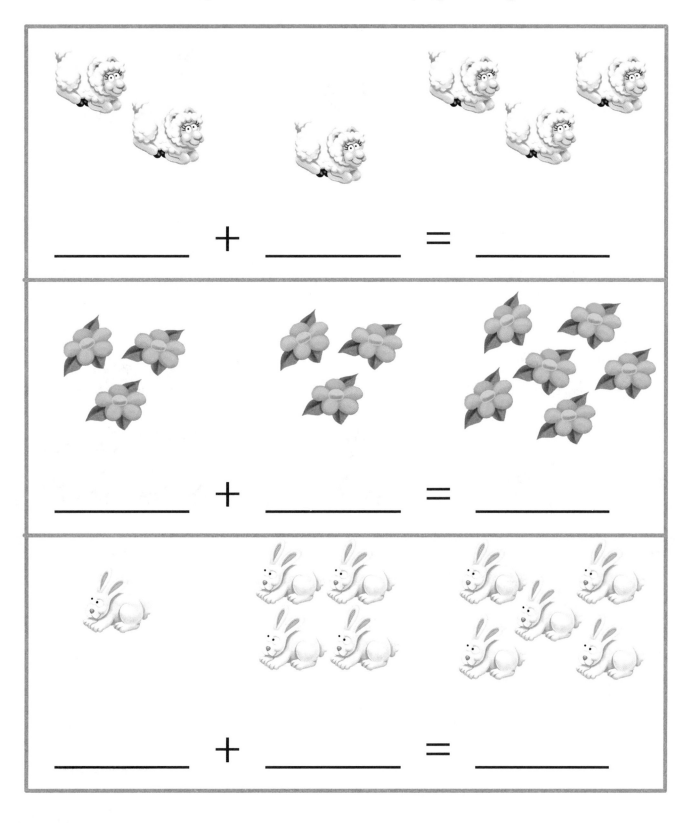

_____ + _____ = _____

_____ + _____ = _____

_____ + _____ = _____

Count on God

God gives us what we need. Count what God has given us. Write how many. Then write how many all together.

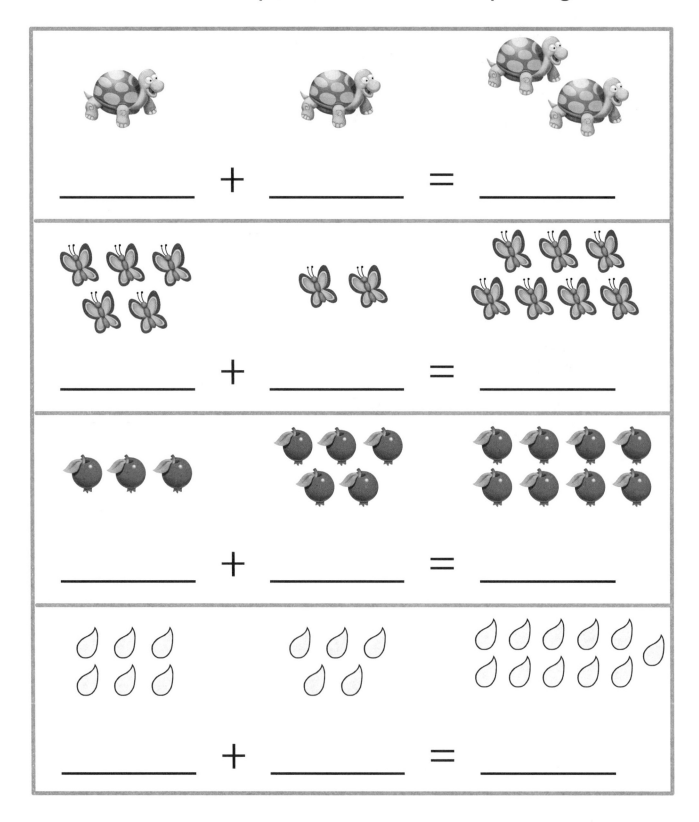

_____ + _____ = _____

_____ + _____ = _____

_____ + _____ = _____

_____ + _____ = _____

Count on God's Love

God gives us what we need. Count what God has given us. Write how many. Then write how many all together.

_____ + _____ = _____

_____ + _____ = _____

_____ + _____ = _____

_____ + _____ = _____

A Pattern of Love

Look at the pattern. Circle what comes next.

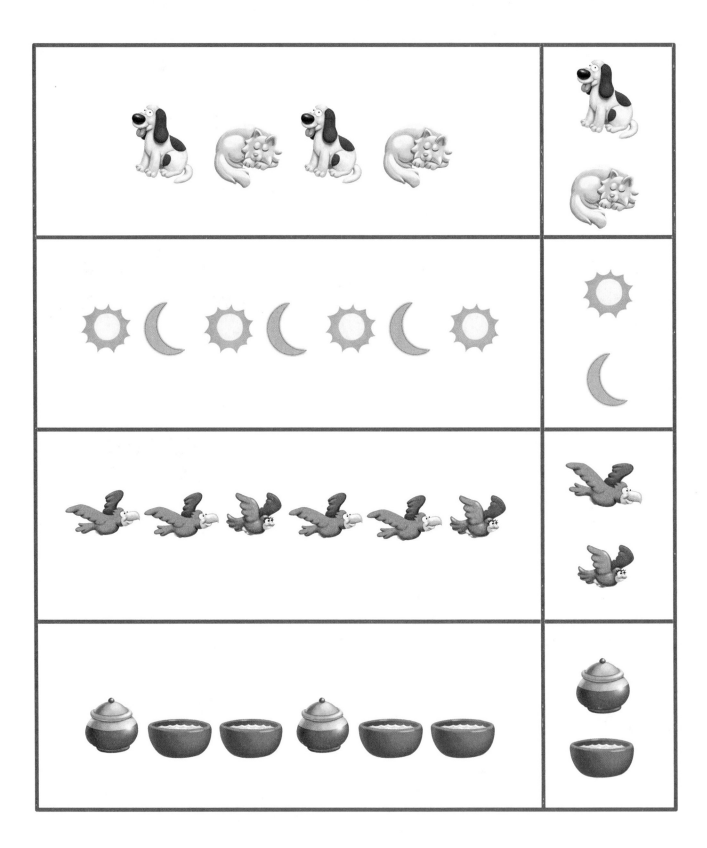

More Patterns

Look at the pattern. Circle what comes next.

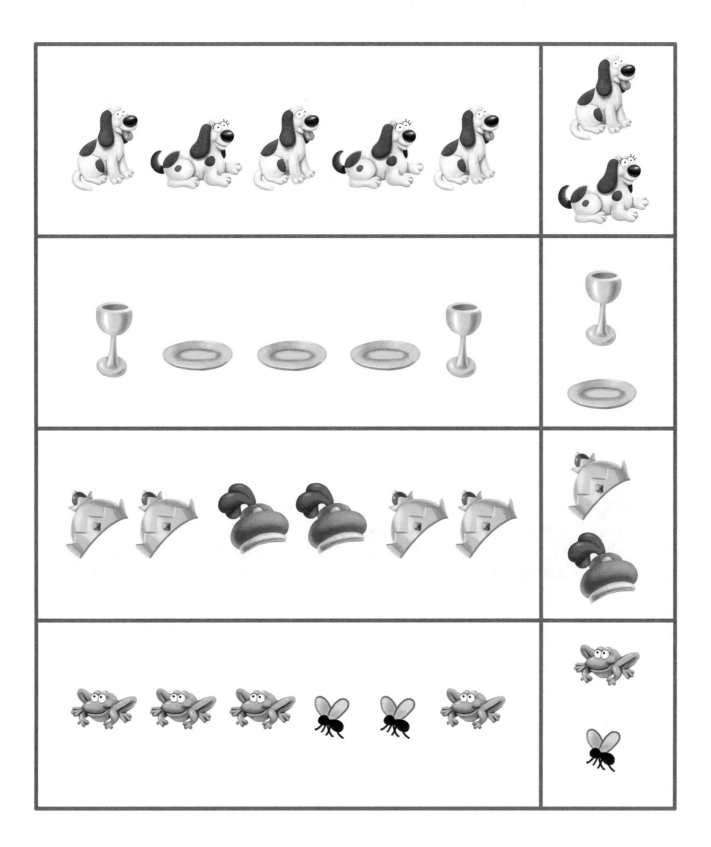

We Love Patterns

God says, "I love you," again and again. Look at the pattern. Circle what comes next.

Perfect Patterns

Look at the pattern. Circle what comes next.

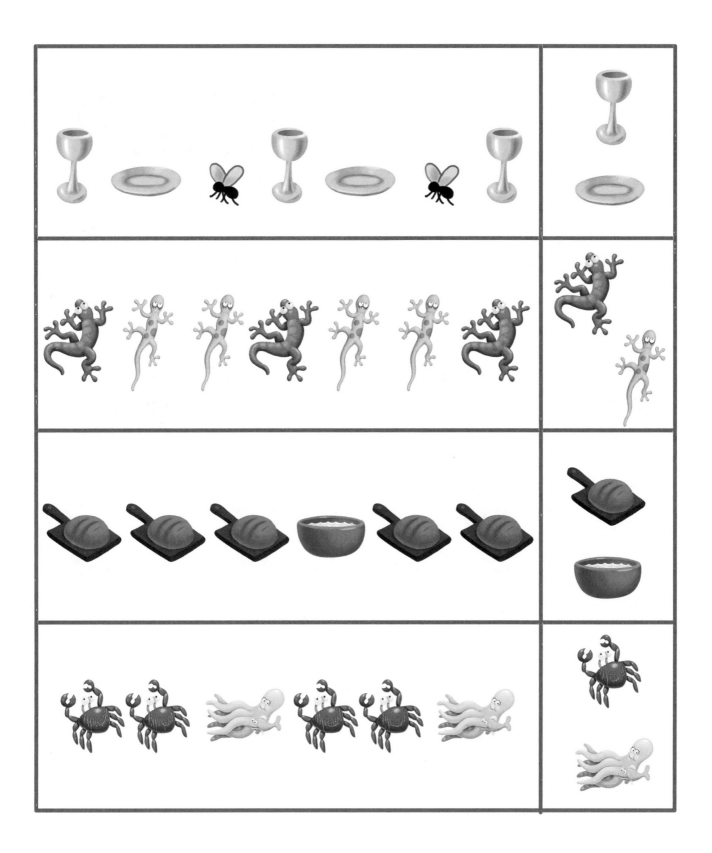

Count on It

We can count on God for everything. Look at the items. Count and answer the questions.

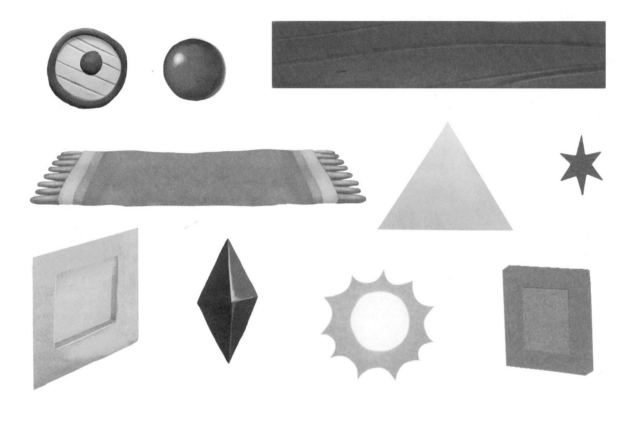

How many ...

are circles? _____

are stars? _____

have 4 sides? _____

Match the Shape

Match the shape. Draw a line.

Dot-to-Dot 1-10

God gave Jacob a wonderful dream. Jacob used his stone pillow to create a reminder. Connect the dots 1-10 to finish the picture.

Dot-to-Dot 1-15

God spoke to Moses through a burning bush.
Connect the dots 1–15 to show the
flames surrounding the bush.

Dot-to-Dot 1-12

The shepherds rushed to Bethlehem. They wanted to meet baby Jesus. Connect the dots 1-12 to make the manger appear.

Count Down

Count. Cross out 1 thing. How many
are left? Write the number.

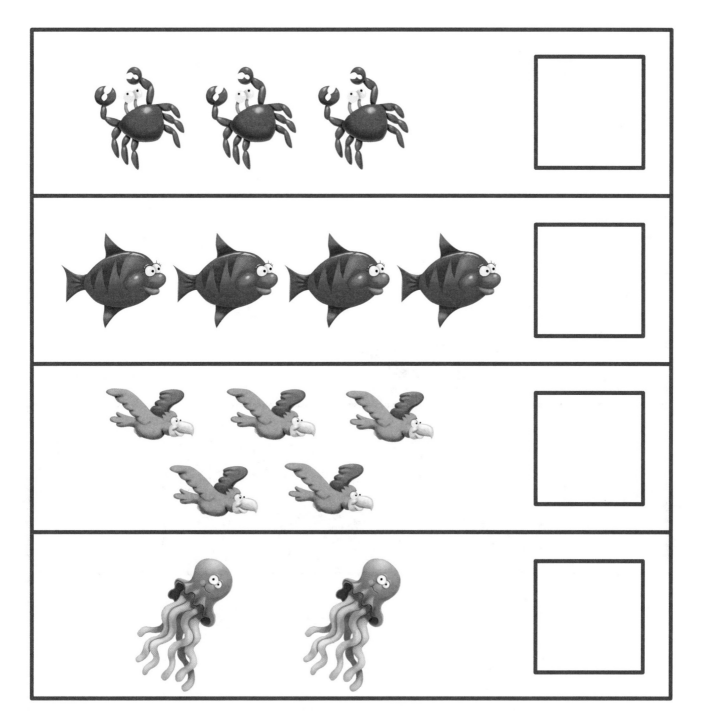

1 2 3 4

How Many Left?

Count. Cross out 1 thing. How many
are left? Write the number.

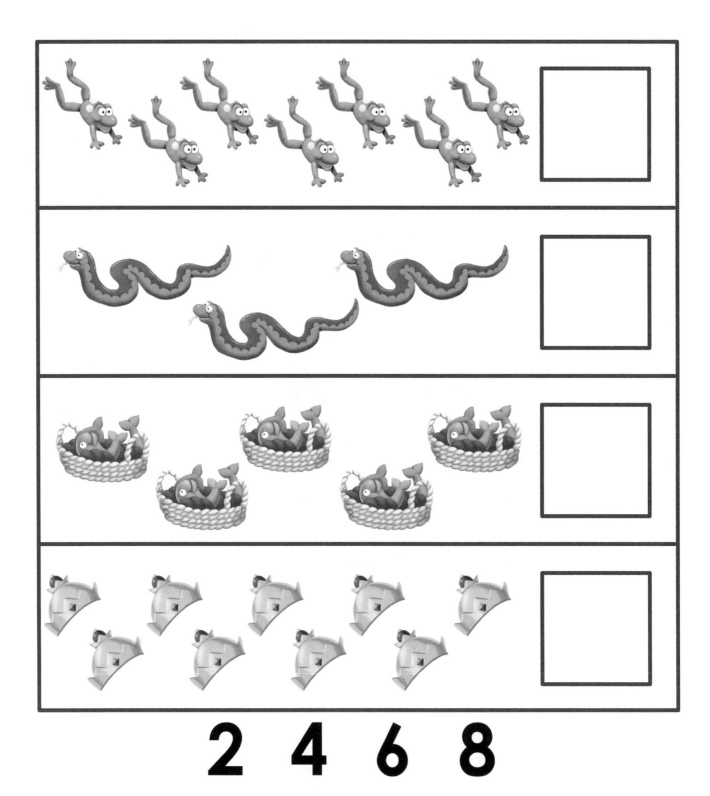

2 4 6 8

One More

Count. Draw one more. Write the number in the box.

Count One More

Count. Draw one more. Write the number in the box.

Count Down

Count. Subtract. Write how many are left.

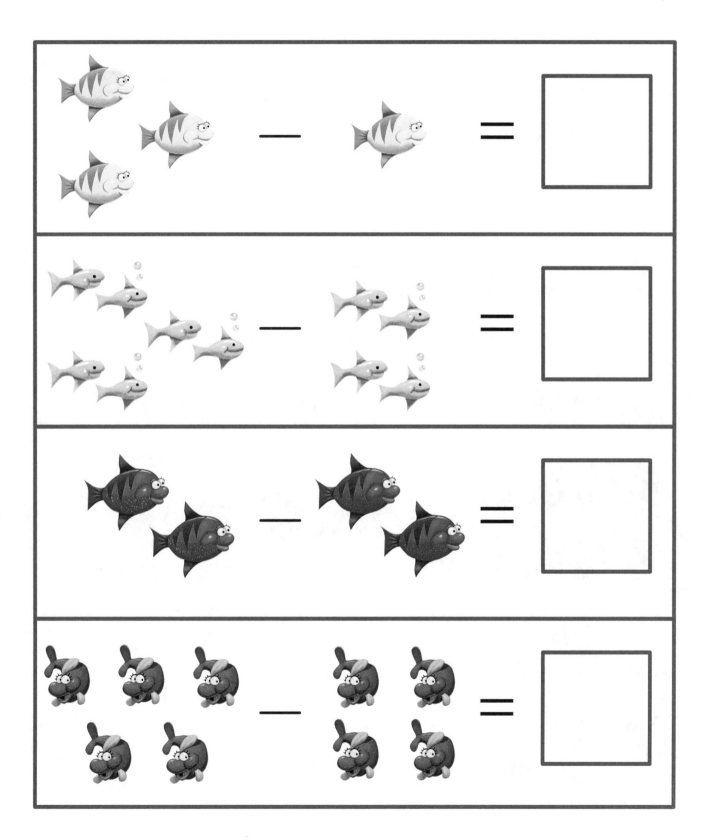

Count Down Again

Count. Subtract. Write how many are left.

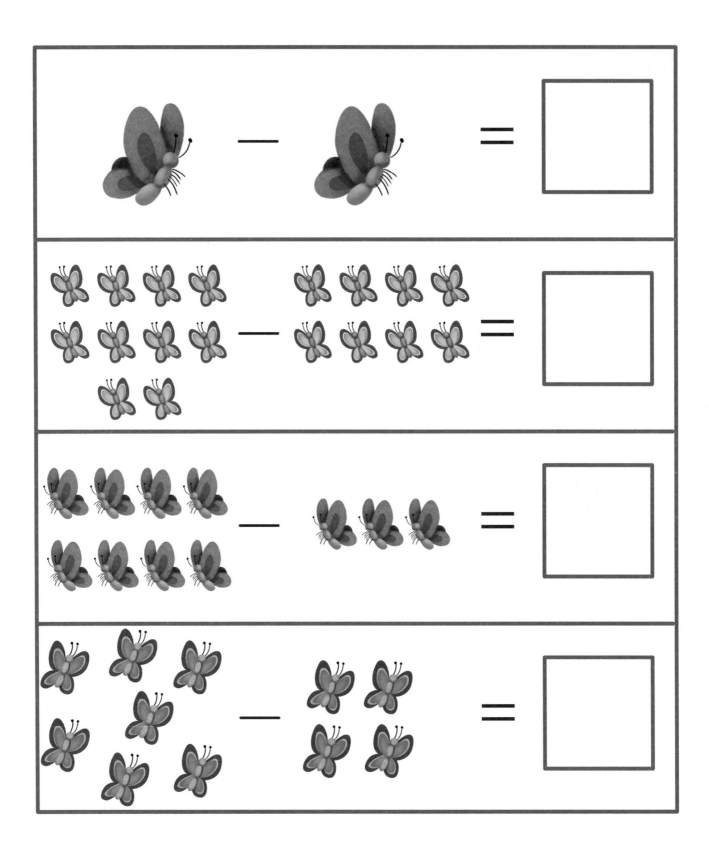

Taking Away

Look at the numbers. Count the cups. Take away. Write the new number of cups. The first one is done for you.

$3 - 1 =$ __2__

$4 - 3 =$ ___

$2 - 1 =$ ___

$5 - 2 =$ ___

$9 - 5 =$ ___

Take It Away

Look at the numbers. Count the moons. Take away. Write the new number of moons. The first one is done for you.

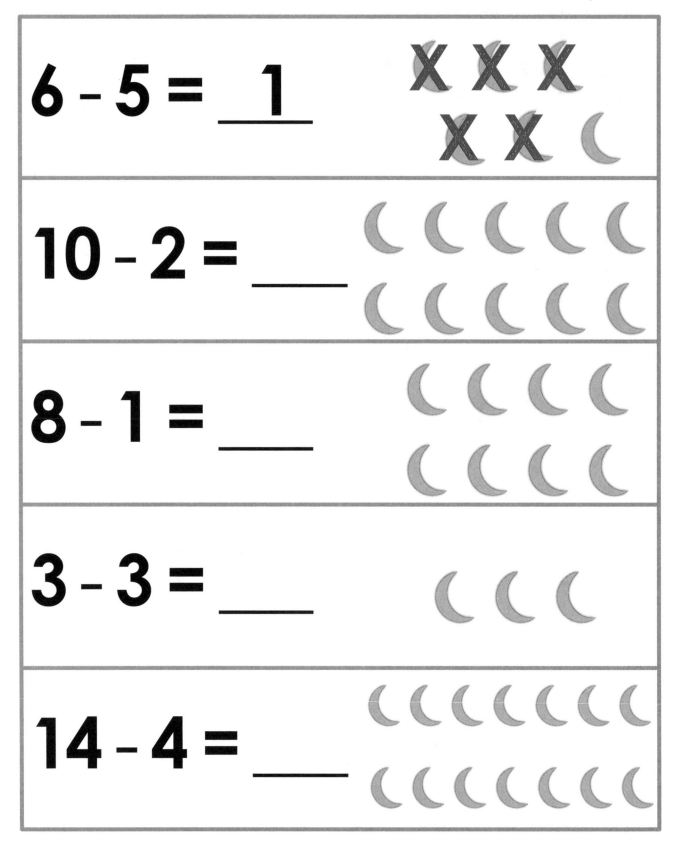

$6 - 5 =$ __1__

$10 - 2 =$ ___

$8 - 1 =$ ___

$3 - 3 =$ ___

$14 - 4 =$ ___

Number Match

Look at the number. Count the items. Look at the word.
Match them with lines. The first one is done for you.

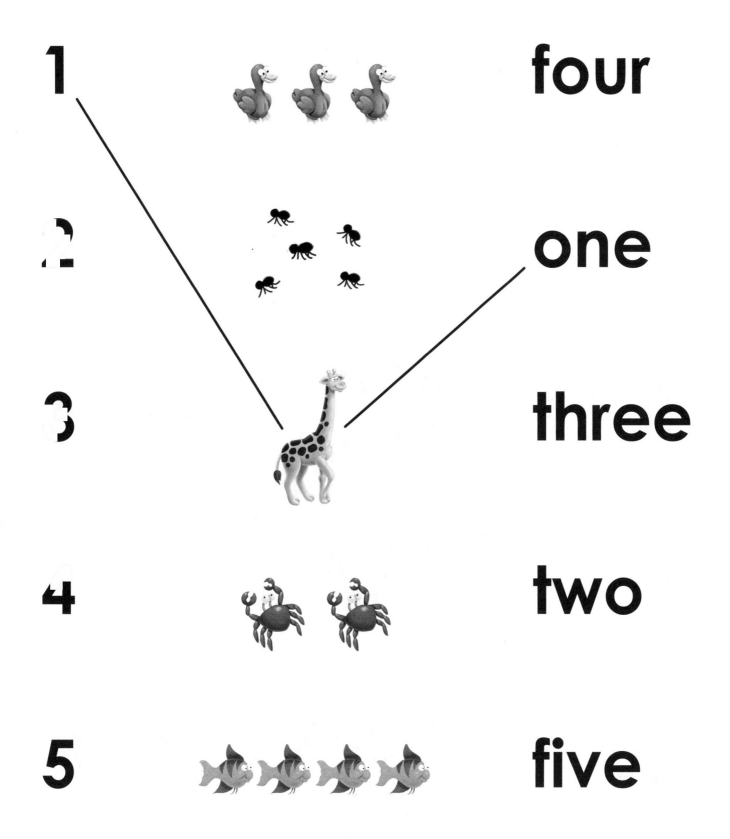

1

2

3

4

5

four

one

three

two

five

Is There a Match?

Look at the number. Count the items. Look at the word.
Match them with lines. The first one is done for you.

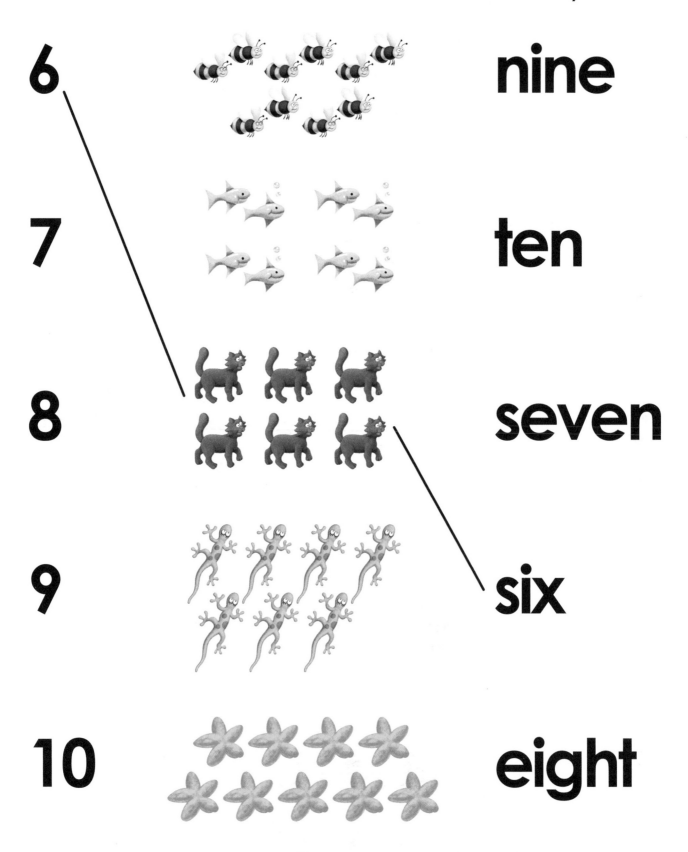

6   nine

7   ten

8   seven

9   six

10   eight

Match Up

Look at the number. Count the items.
Look at the word. Match them with lines.

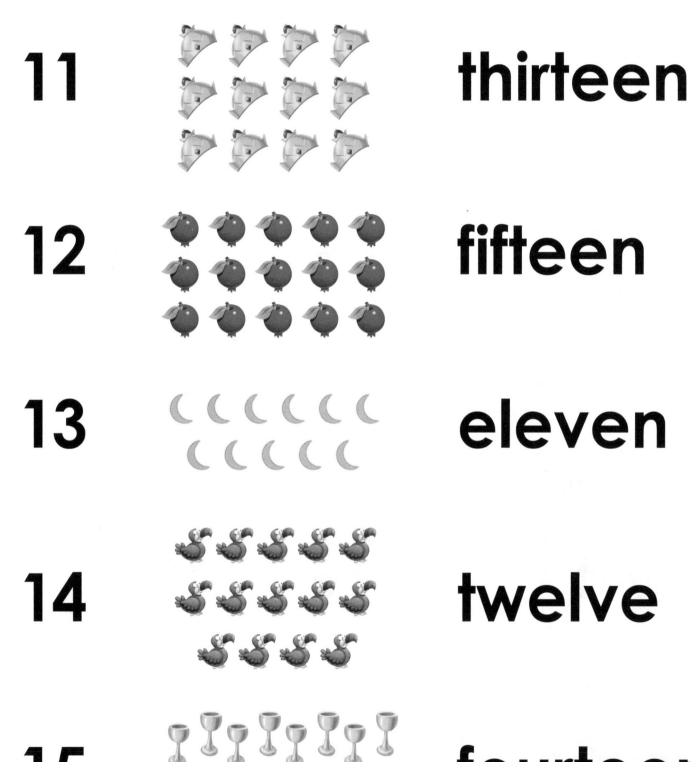

11

12

13

14

15

thirteen

fifteen

eleven

twelve

fourteen

You Are Number One

Add 1 to the number in each sun. Write
the new number in the cloud.

3 + 1 =

5 + 1 =

8 + 1 =

4 + 1 =

2 + 1 =

Count It

Look at the number. Count the penguins.
Add. Write the new number.

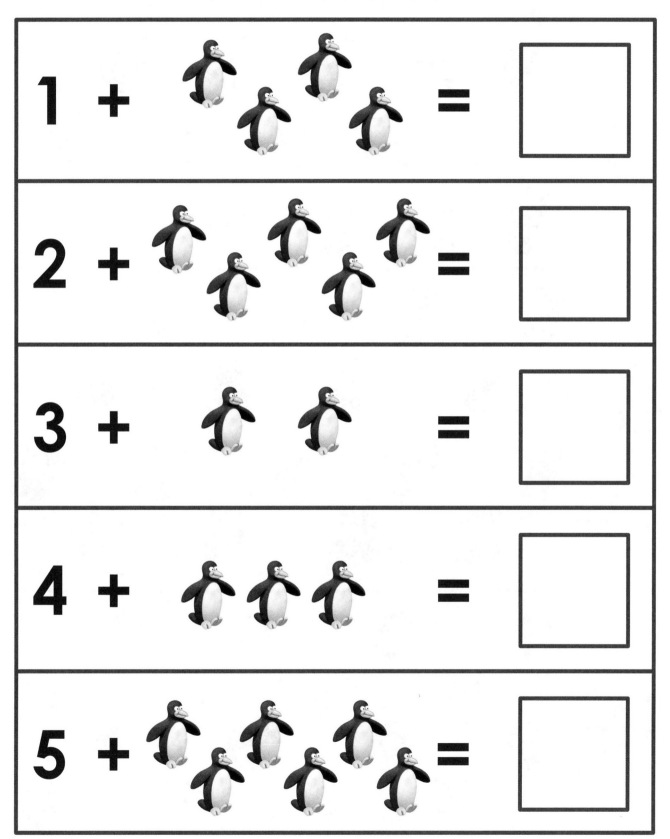

Cross It Out

Look at the number. Put an X on the correct number of items. The first one is done for you.

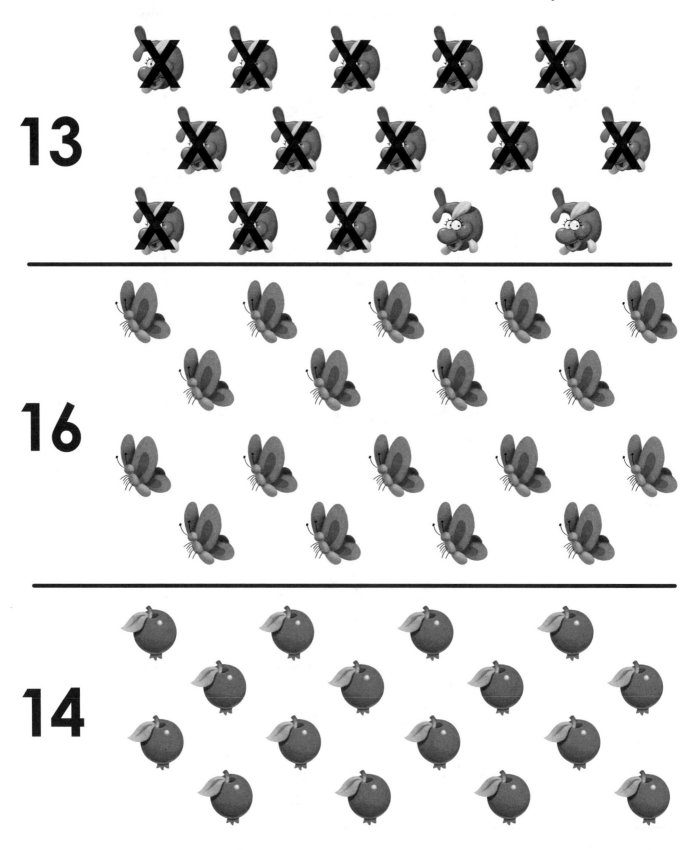

13

16

14

Count It Out

Look at the number. Put an X on the correct number of items. The first one is done for you.

20

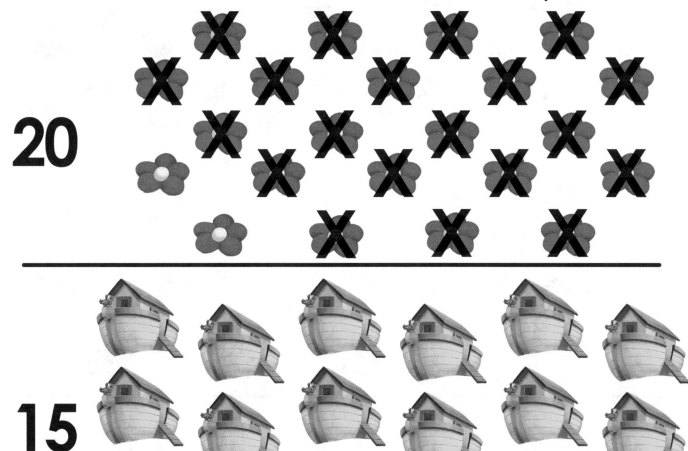

15

12

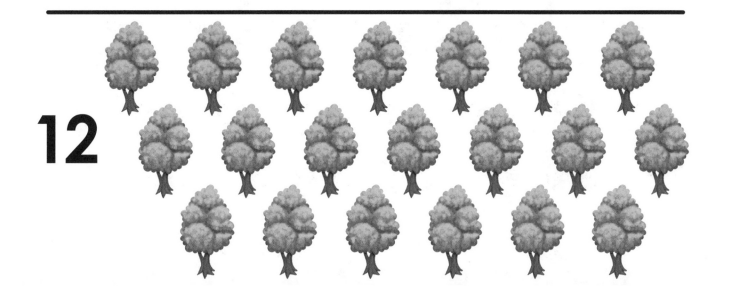

X It

Look at the number. Put an X on the correct number of items.

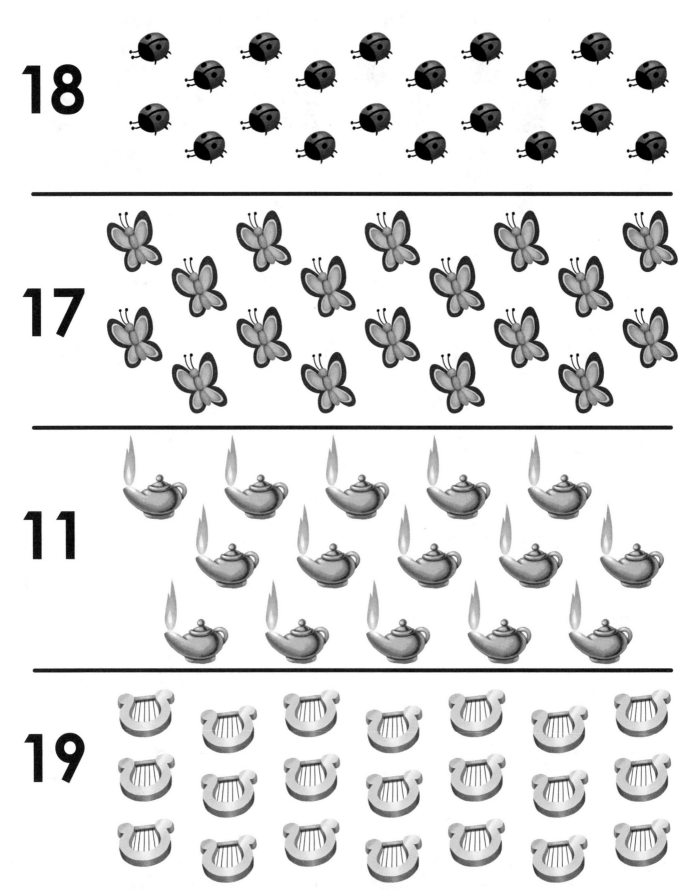

18

17

11

19

Help Noah!

Help Noah get to the ark before it rains. Find the path from 1 to 10. Color the boxes. The path is started for you.

	8	10	4	5	3	10
→	1	2	3	6	8	3
10	5	9	6	4	7	9	5
1	3	4	2	6	8	1	4
8	10	1	9	6	9	
2	2	7	10	9	10	

Where Are My Sheep?

Help the shepherd find his sheep. Find the path from 1 to 12. Color the boxes. The path is started for you.

		1	5	7	6	11	12
		2	9	2	3	10	11
8	9	3	4	5	6	7	4
2	8	5	3	10	9	8	10
2	6	6	7	11	12		
11	7	11	9	1	7		

Jonah's Fish

Where is the big fish? Help Jonah find him fast! Find the path from 1 to 15. Color the boxes. The path is started for you.

	13	9	4	4	11	6
	8	9	10	3	12	7
1	14	7	3	11	6	9	5
2	15	6	7	12	8	10	8
3	4	5	8	13	5	
9	8	1	3	14	15	

God's Love Is BIG

God loves all his creation!
♡ the small ones in red. X the medium ones
in blue. Circle the big ones in green.

God Loves All Things

Big and small, God loves it all!
♡ the small ones in red. X the medium ones in
blue. Circle the big ones in green.

Jesus and His Happy Friends

Here is Jesus! Here are his friends. Read and then count. Write the number.

Count how many men. . . . . _____

How many feet do you see? . . . . _____

How many eyes do you see? . . . . _____

Count how many are wearing red. . . . . _____

Count how many smiles. . . . . _____

Many People Get Baptized

People loved Jesus. They got baptized. Read and then count. Write the number.

Count how many people all together. . . _____

How many people are in the water?. . . . _____

Count how many children . . . . _____

Count how many flowers . . . . _____

Count how many eyes you see. . . . . _____

God Made Every Animal Good!

Count. How many are there?

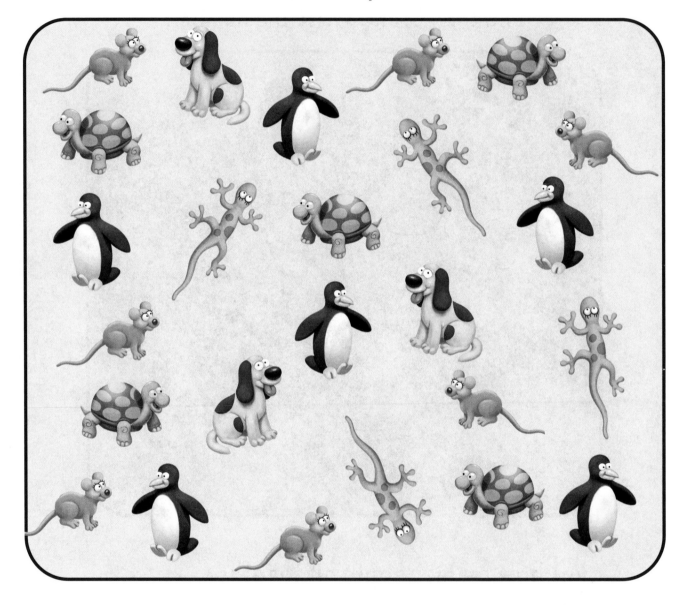

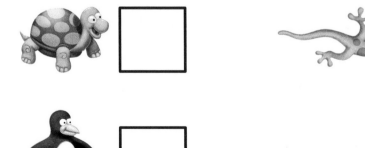

Count Up God's Creations

Count. How many are there?

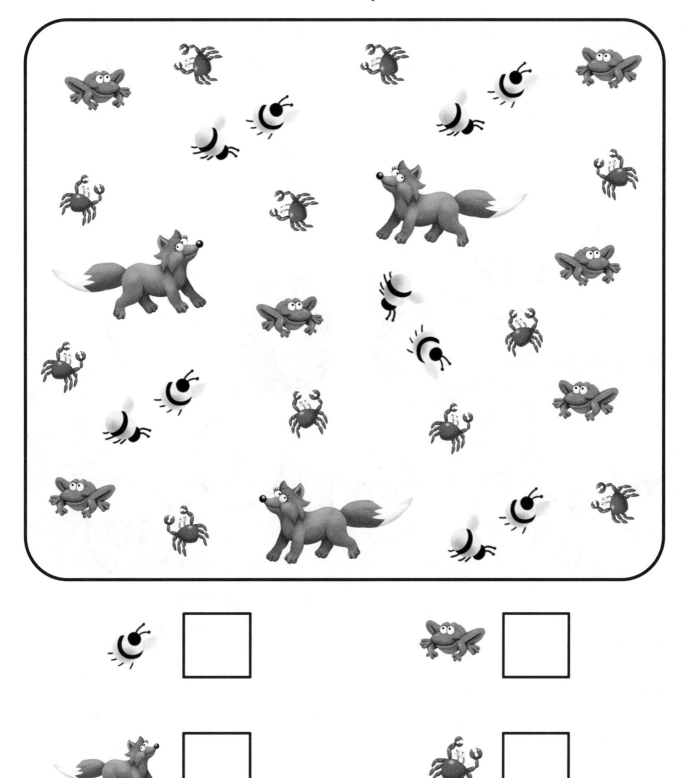

Color the Number 10

Look for 10. Color each 10 red.

Color the Number 11

Look for 11. Color each 11 green.

Color the Number 12

Look for 12. Color each 12 blue.

Color the Number 13

Look for 13. Color each 13 yellow.

Color the Number 14

Look for 14. Color each 14 red.

Color the Number 15

Look for 15. Color each 15 orange.

Color the Number 16

Look for 16. Color each 16 brown.

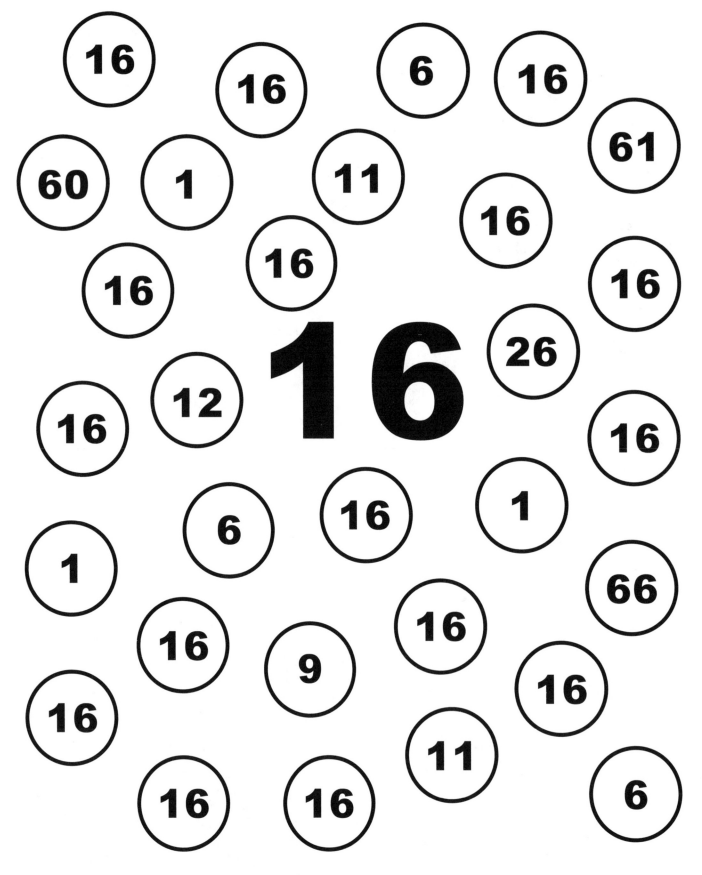

Color the Number 17

Look for 17. Color each 17 green.

Color the Number 18

Look for 18. Color each 18 purple.

Color the Number 19

Look for 19. Color each 19 red.

Color the Number 20

Look for 20. Color each 20 yellow.

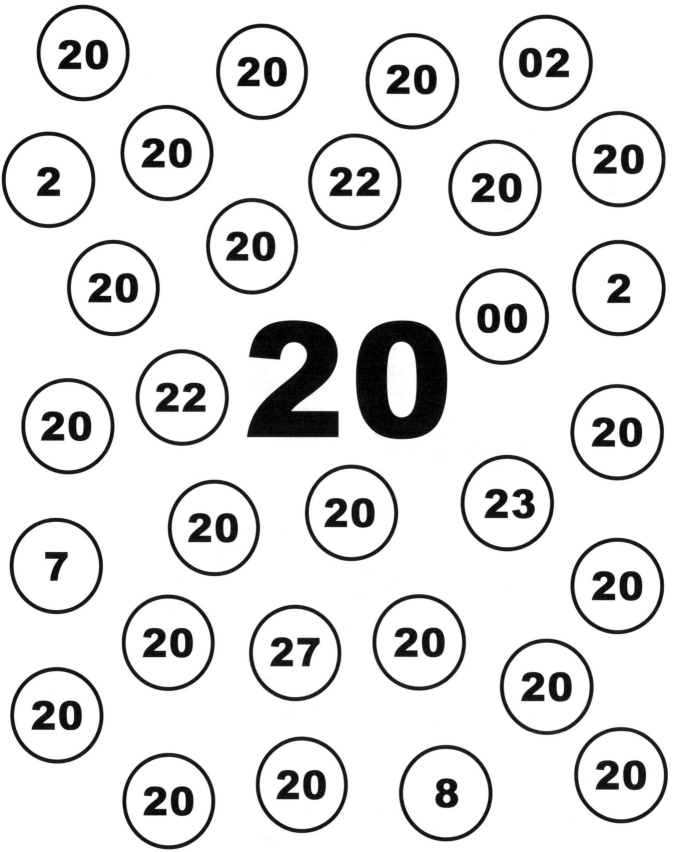

Counting Legs

God gave lambs 4 legs.

How many legs do 2 lambs have?

_____

How many legs do 4 lambs have?

_____

How many legs do 6 lambs have?

_____

How many legs do 3 lambs have?

_____

How many legs do 5 lambs have?

_____

Lots of Apples

God made apples grow on trees.

How many apples on 5 trees?

_____

How many apples on 4 trees?

_____

How many apples on 3 trees?

_____

How many apples on 2 trees?

_____

How many apples on 1 tree?

_____

Graphing God's Gifts

Look at some of God's gifts to us. Count. Color a box for each item you find. The first one is done for you.

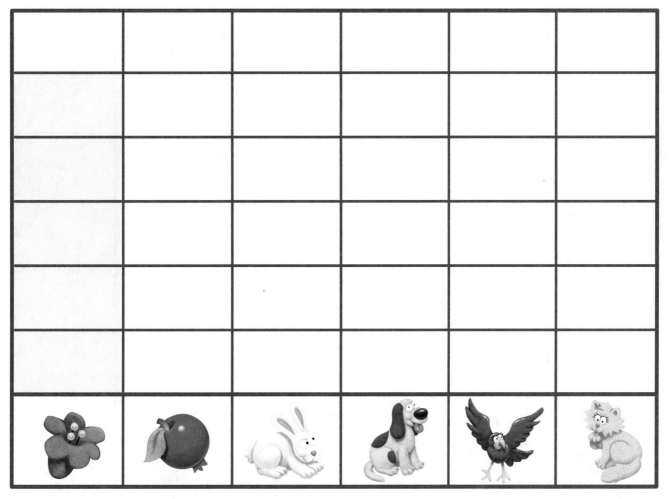

Graph Everyday Things

Look at these everyday things. Count.
Color a box for each thing you find.

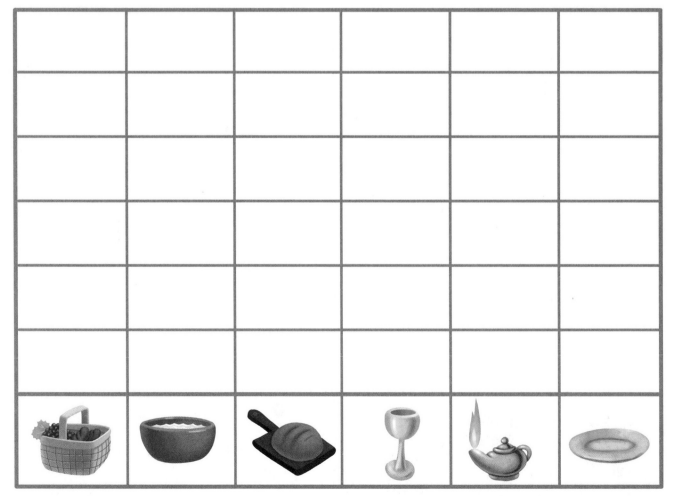

Graphing All Good Things

God created everything and said, "It is good!" Look at these good things. Count. Color a box for each thing you find.

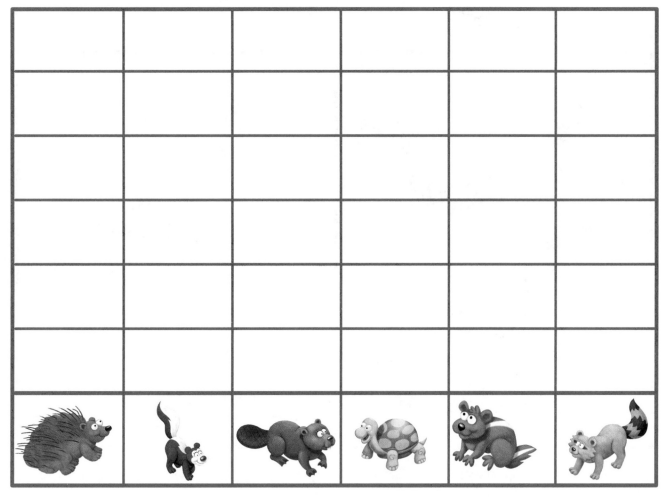

Look for the Longest

Circle the longest in each box.

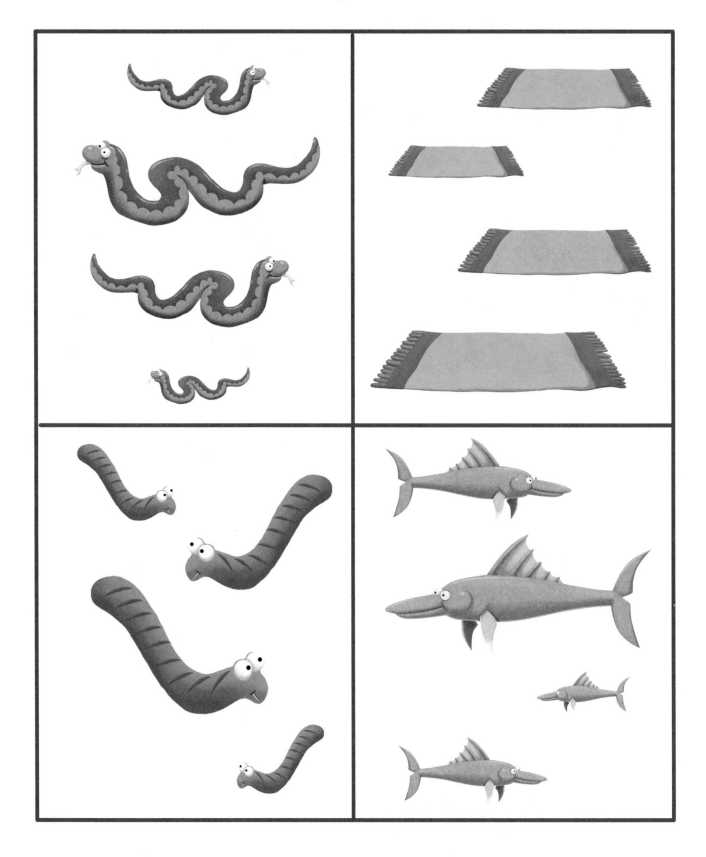

All Shapes and Sizes

Circle the longest in each box.

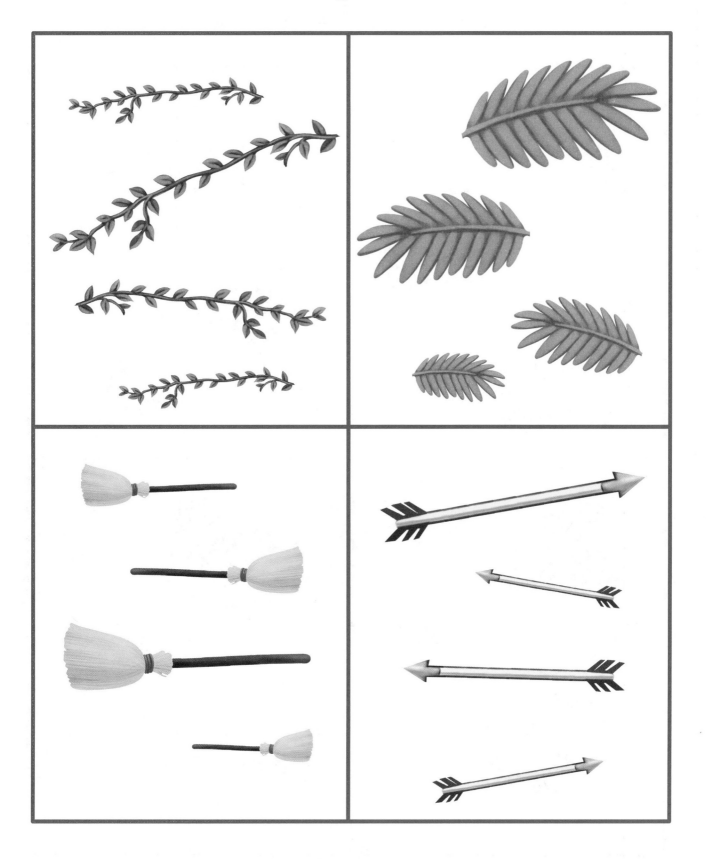

Big or Small

Big or small, God loves it all.
Circle the biggest. X the smallest.

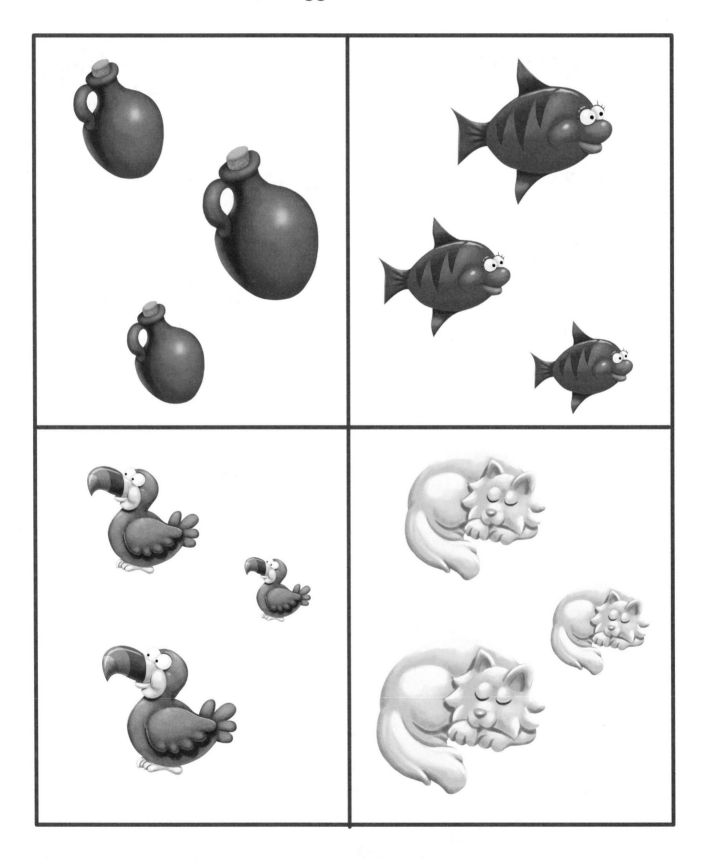

Big or Little

Big or little, God loves it all.
Circle the biggest. X the smallest.

Which One Is Bigger?

God made big things. God made small things.
Circle the BIG thing.

Big and Small

God made big things. God made small things.
Circle the SMALL thing.

God Made the Ocean!

Look in the water God made. Draw and color:
- **3** fish
- **5** jellyfish
- **6** starfish

Let's Go Outside

Thank you, God, for nature! Draw and color:
- **4** clouds
- **7** children
- **9** flowers
- **1** sun

A Hot Desert

God made deserts hot. Draw and color:

- **1** sun
- **2** camels
- **6** cups of water
- **3** snakes

Jesus Rides a Donkey

Jesus rode a donkey when he went to Jerusalem.
Connect the dots counting from 1-40 to finish the picture.

Noah's Big Boat

God told Noah how to build the ark. It was a very big boat!
Connect the dots counting from 1–20 to finish the picture.

Joseph's Colorful Coat

Joseph's dad gave him a colorful coat.
Color the picture. Use the color key.

1 = green   2 = blue   3 = yellow   4 = red   5 = purple   6 = brown   7 = tan

God's Colorful Creation

Color God's creation. Use the color key.

1=blue   2=brown   3=green   4=red   5=yellow   6=purple

Adam & Eve Love Animals

Color Adam and Eve with animals. Use the color key.

1=blue 2=brown 3=green 4=red 5=yellow

6=purple 7=tan 8=white 9=pink

Color Moses

God gave Moses the Ten Commandments on two big stones.
Color Moses and the Ten Commandments. Use the color key.

1 = gray   2 = purple   3 = brown   4 = orange   5 = pink   6 = tan

Meet Jonah

Jonah did not listen to God. God sent a big fish to teach Jonah.
Color Jonah and the fish. Use the color key.

1 = blue   2 = yellow   3 = brown   4 = orange   5 = pink   6 = tan   7 = purple

Dot-to-Dot 1-20

God made the trees on the ground. He made clouds in the sky! Connect the dots counting from 1-20 to finish the picture. Now color it.

Trace These

God made everything just right!
Trace the shape.

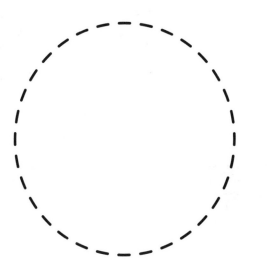

God made the
sun a circle.

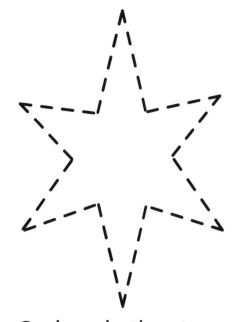

God made the stars.

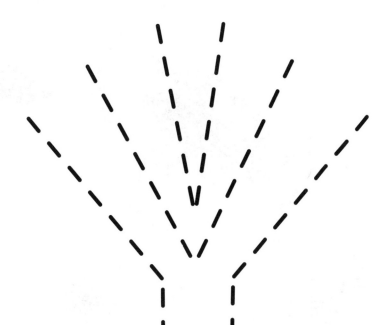

God made tall trees.

Count and Sort

Look at the animals God created with wings and with fur.
Match the animal to the right category. Then count how many.

How many animals with fur? _____

How many animals with wings? _____

Sort These Out

Look at things God made. Match the item to the right category.
Then count how many.

How many people? _____

How many plants that grow? _____

Count and Compare
God's Animals

Count the things. Write the numbers in the boxes. X the things that have the most in each row. The first one is done for you.

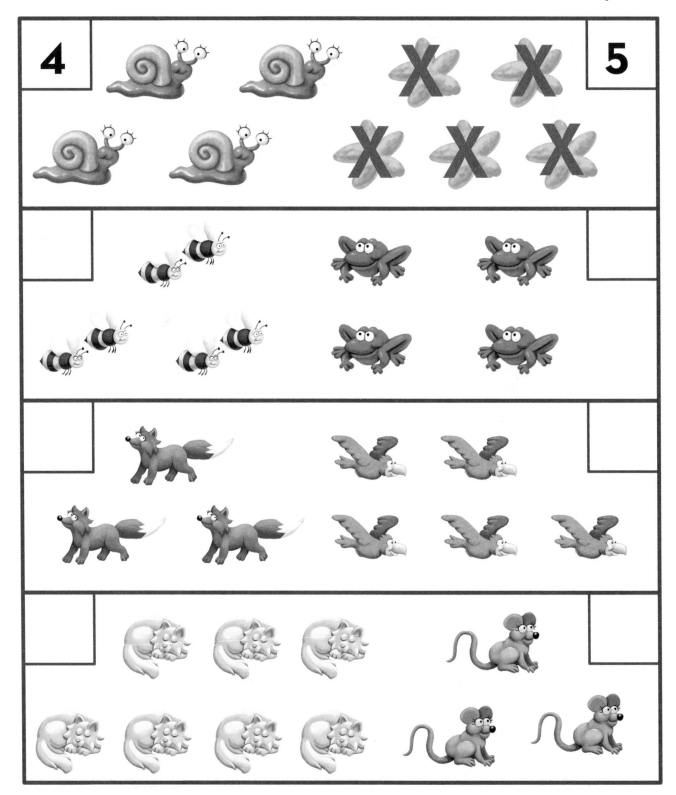

Count and Compare God's Creation

Count the things. Write the numbers in the boxes. X the things that have the most in each row. The first one is done for you.

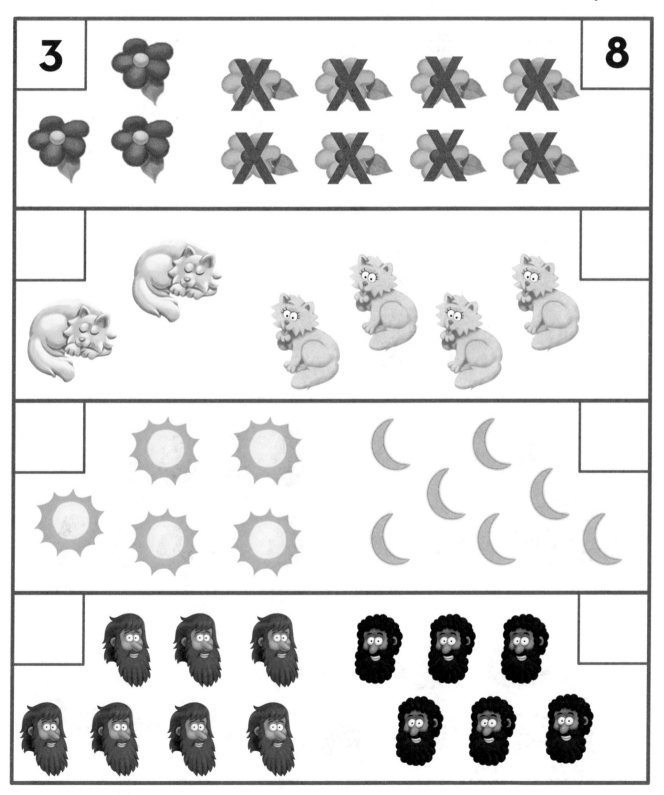

Count and Compare
All Around

Count the things. Write the numbers in the boxes.
X the things that have the most in each row.

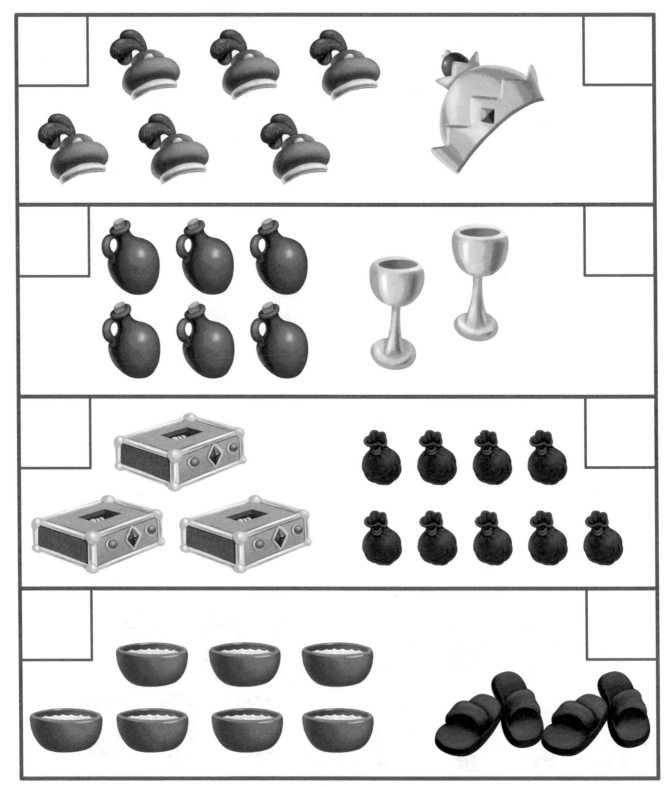

Match Up

Look at the numbers and the words. Match the star with the correct sheep. The first one is done for you.

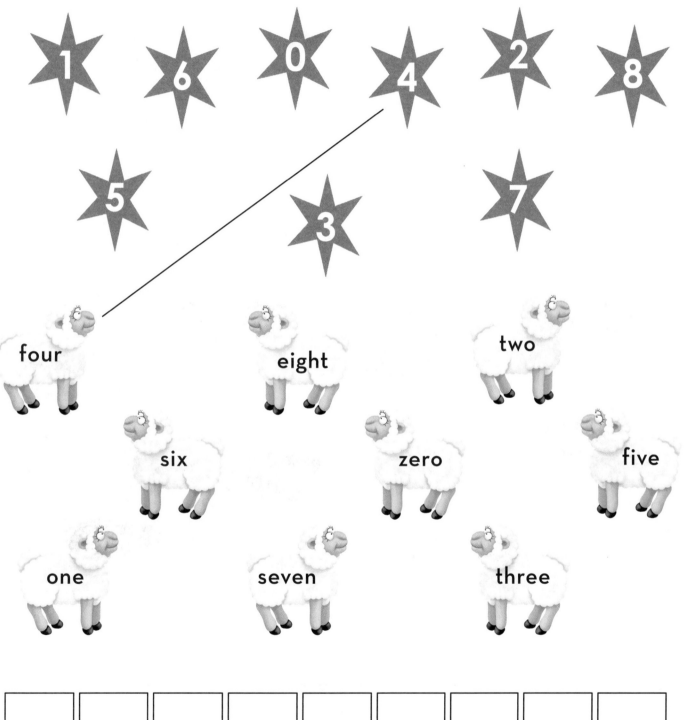

Now, write 0-8 in the boxes.

Match ´Em

Look at the numbers and the words. Match the cup with the correct bread. The first one is done for you.

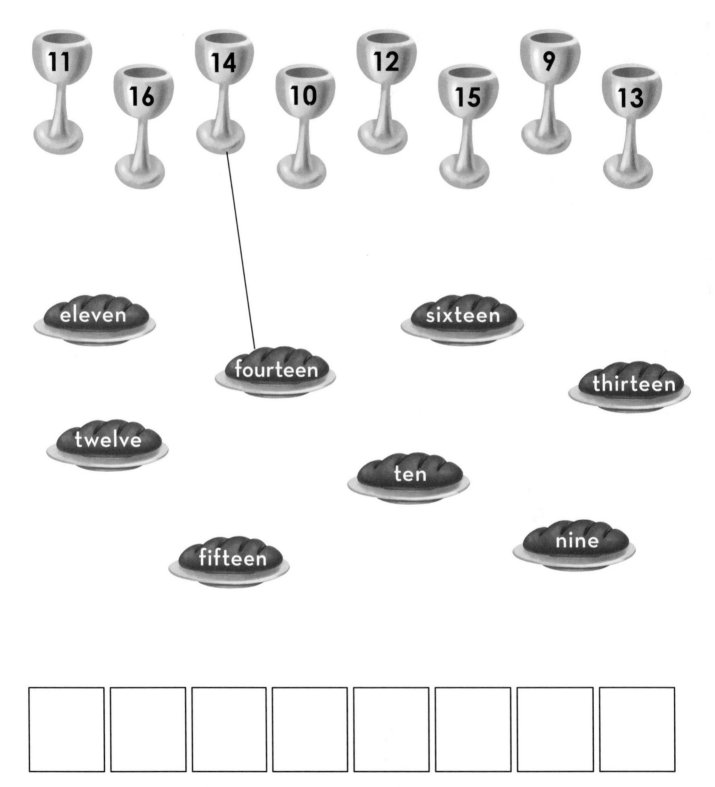

Now, write 9–16 in the boxes.

Can Moses Make It?

Help Moses find the Ten Commandments. Then help Moses find the promised land. Trace the paths.

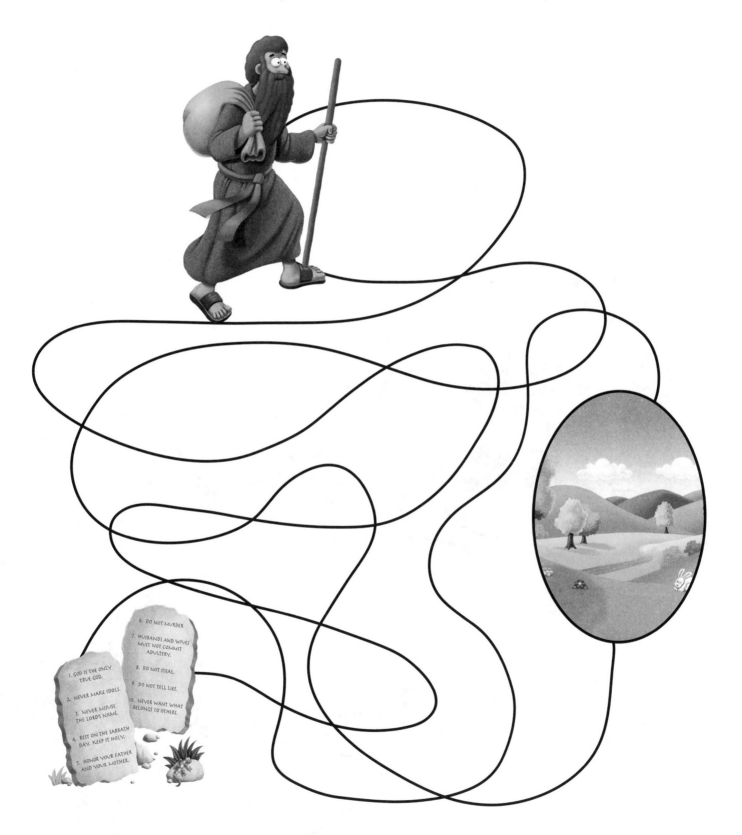

Where Is My Donkey?

Jesus needs a donkey to ride. He is going to see his friends.
Help Jesus find his donkey and then his friends. Trace the paths.

Where Is the Water?

God made fish and other animals to swim in the water.
Help these animals find the water. Trace the paths.

Sets of One

Circle all the sets of one sun.

Sets of Two

Circle all the sets of two snakes.

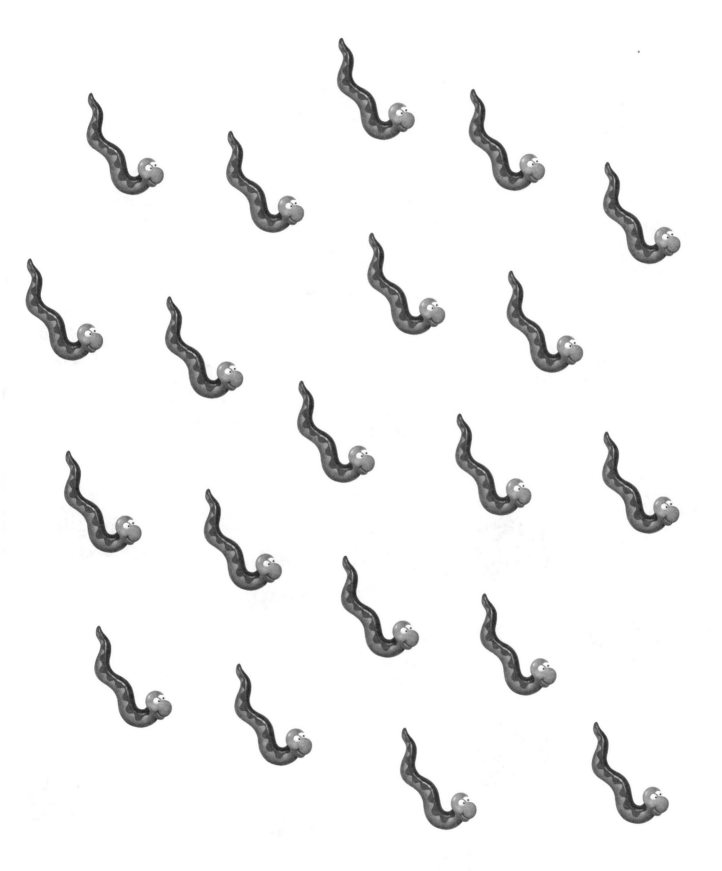

Sets of Three

Circle all the sets of three flowers.

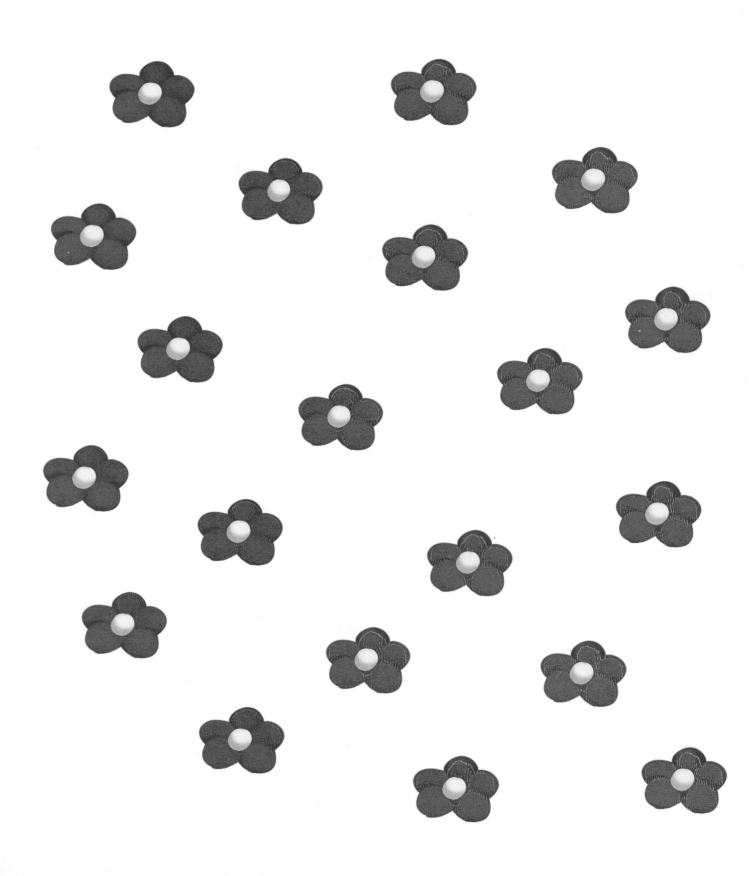

Sets of Four

Circle all the sets of four bunnies.

Sets of Five

Circle all the sets of five arks.

Sets of Six

Circle all the sets of six dogs.

Sets of Seven

Circle all the sets of seven birds.

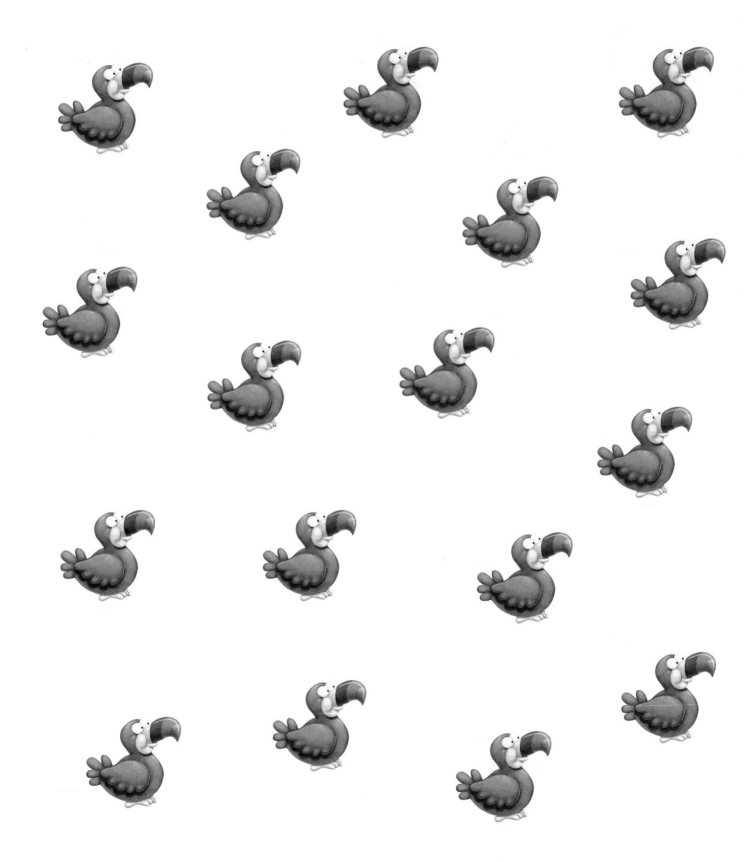

Sets of Eight

Circle all the sets of eight cats.

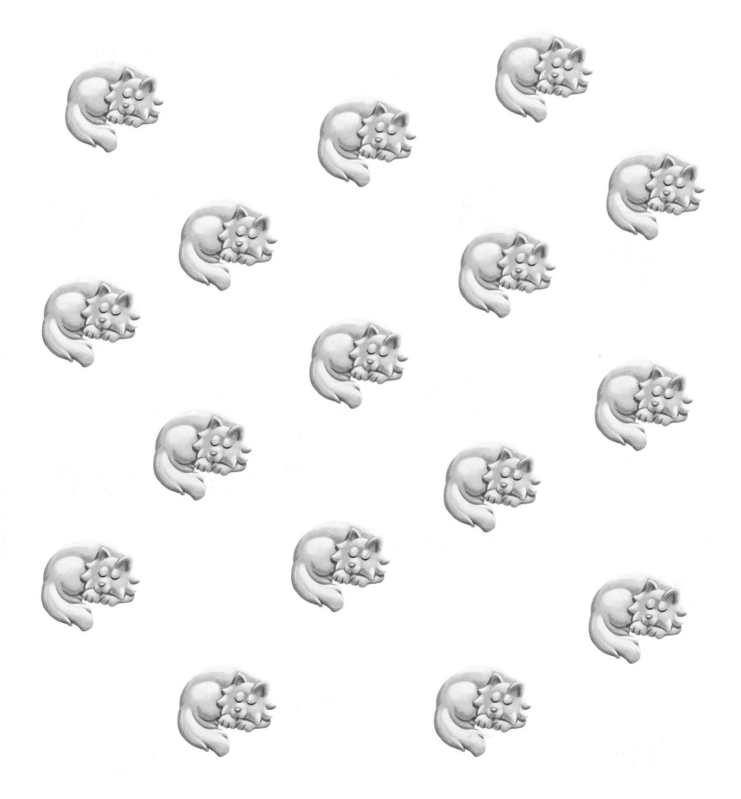

Sets of Nine

Circle all the sets of nine frogs.

Sets of Ten

Circle all the sets of ten bugs.

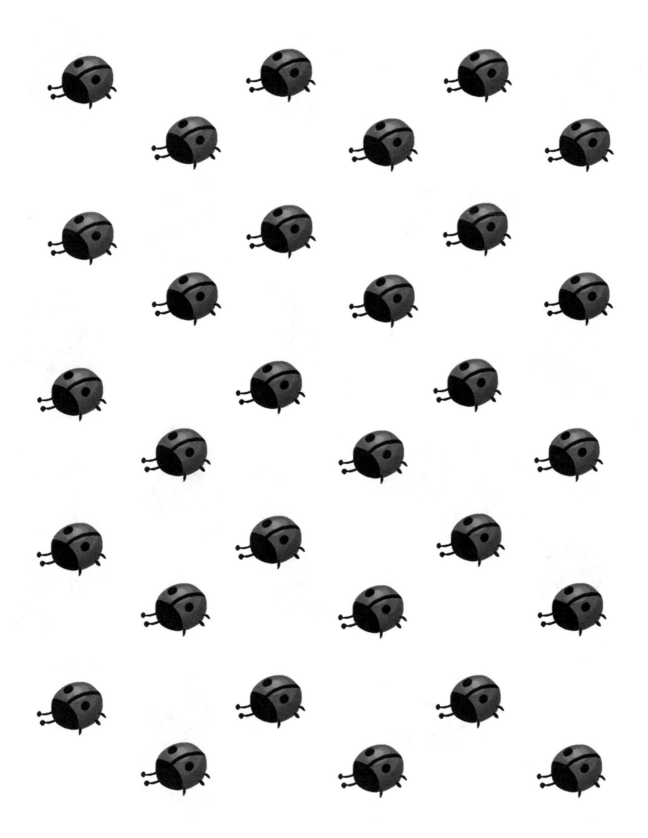

Sets of Eleven

Circle all the sets of eleven lions.

Sets of Twelve

Circle all the sets of twelve lamps.

Sets of Thirteen

Circle all the sets of thirteen moons.

Sets of Fourteen

Circle all the sets of fourteen crowns.

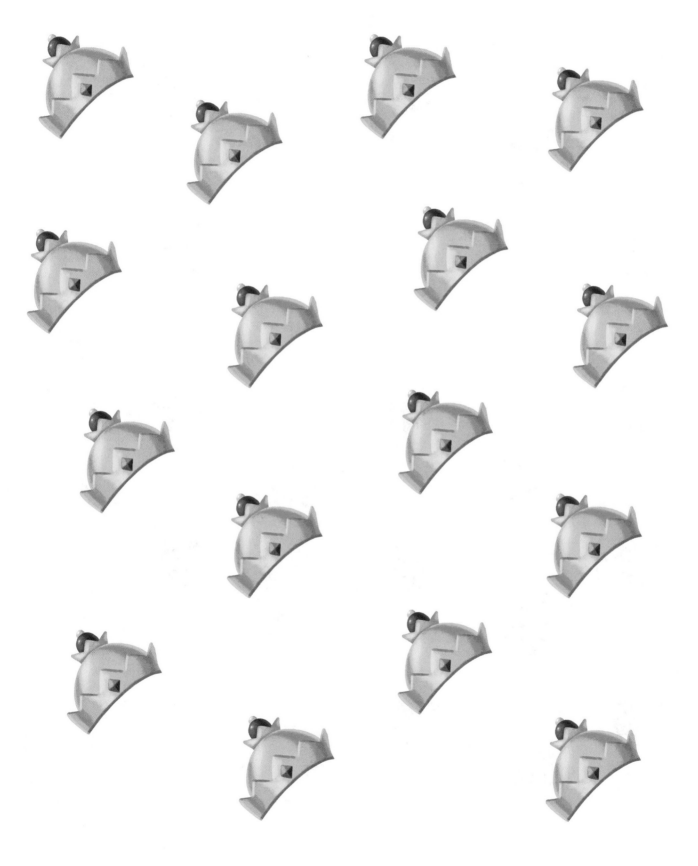

Sets of Fifteen

Circle all the sets of fifteen fish.

More and More

Touch the objects as you count each group.
Circle the group with more.

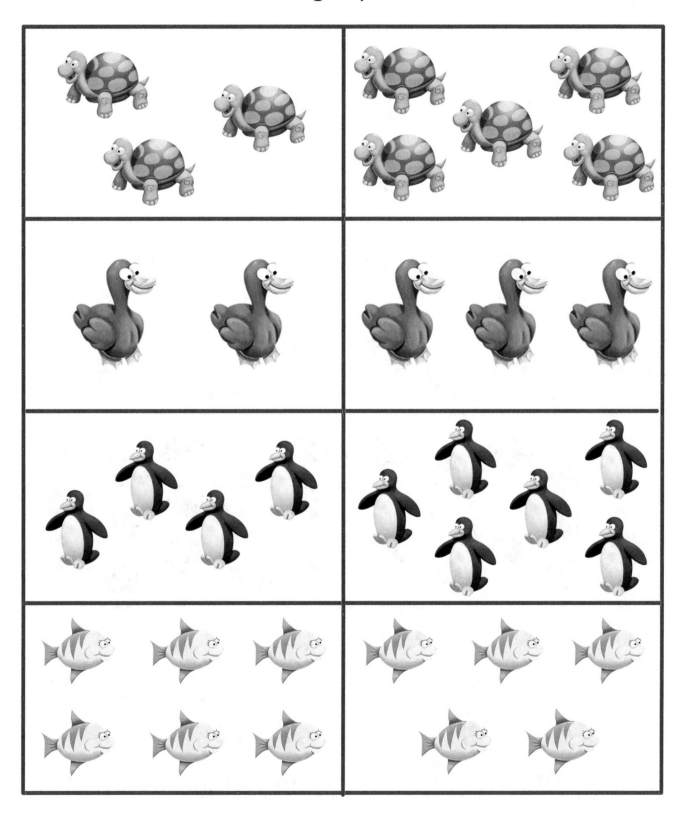

More Than the Other

Touch the objects as you count each group.
Circle the group with more.

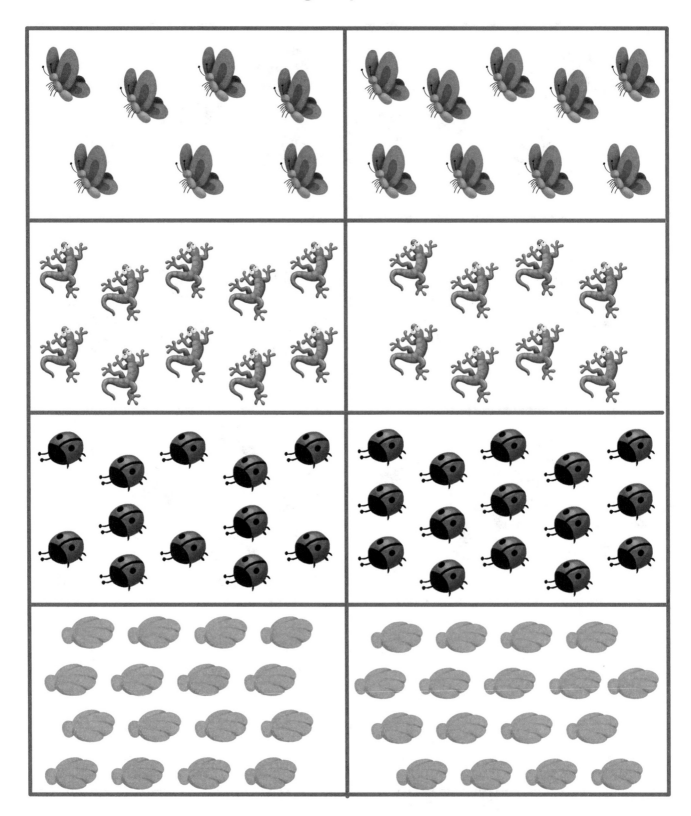

Which Is Greater Than?

Circle the number that is greater in each set.
The first one is done for you.

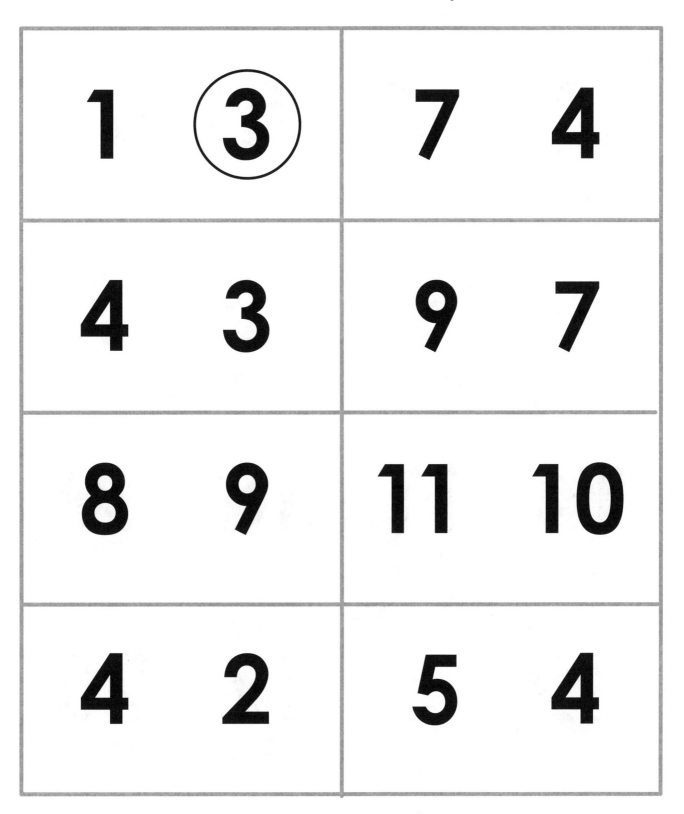

Greater Than

Circle the number that is greater in each set.

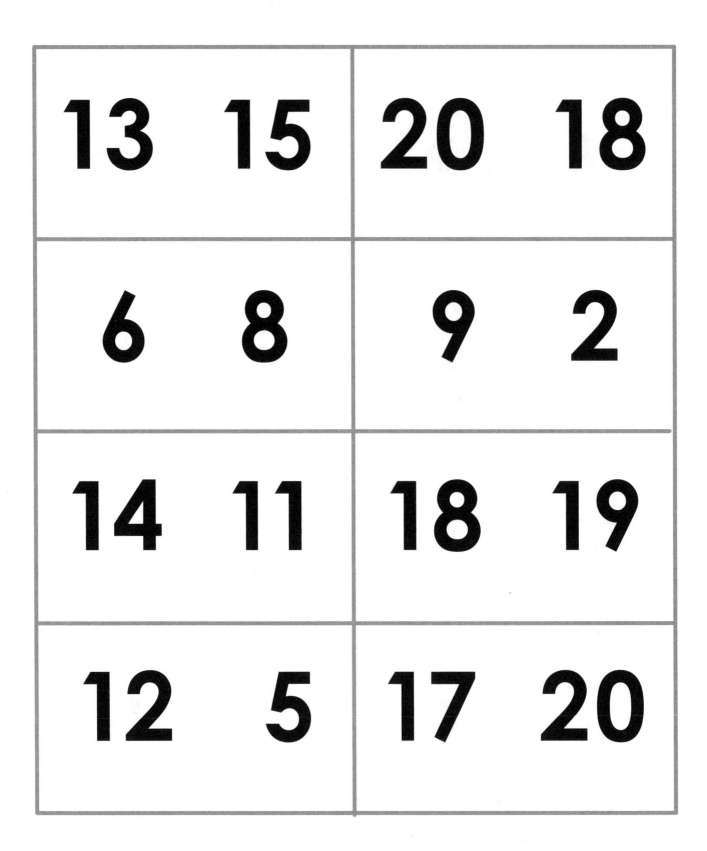

13 15	20 18
6 8	9 2
14 11	18 19
12 5	17 20

Less Than

Circle the number that is less in each set.
The first one is done for you.

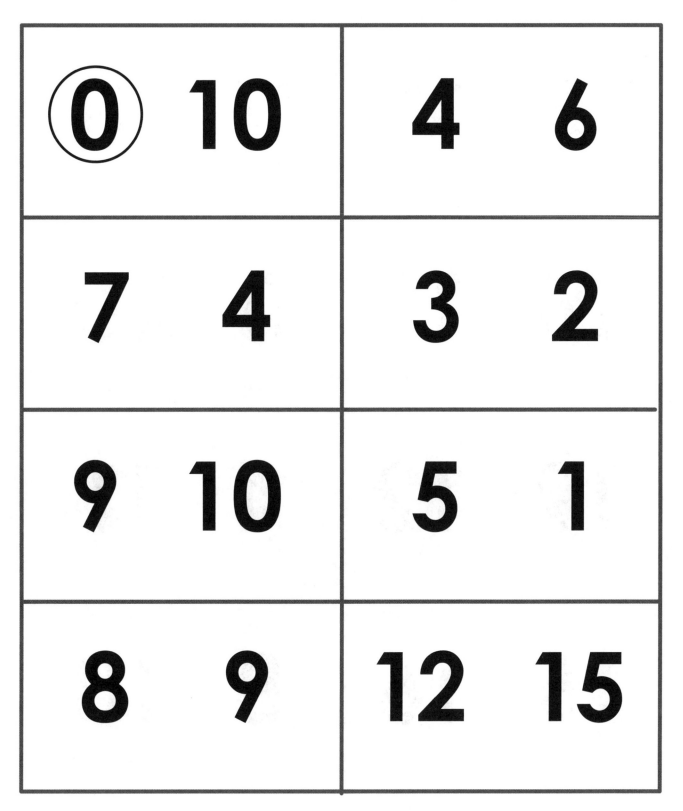

⓪ 10	4 6
7 4	3 2
9 10	5 1
8 9	12 15

Which Is Less?

Circle the number that is less in each set.

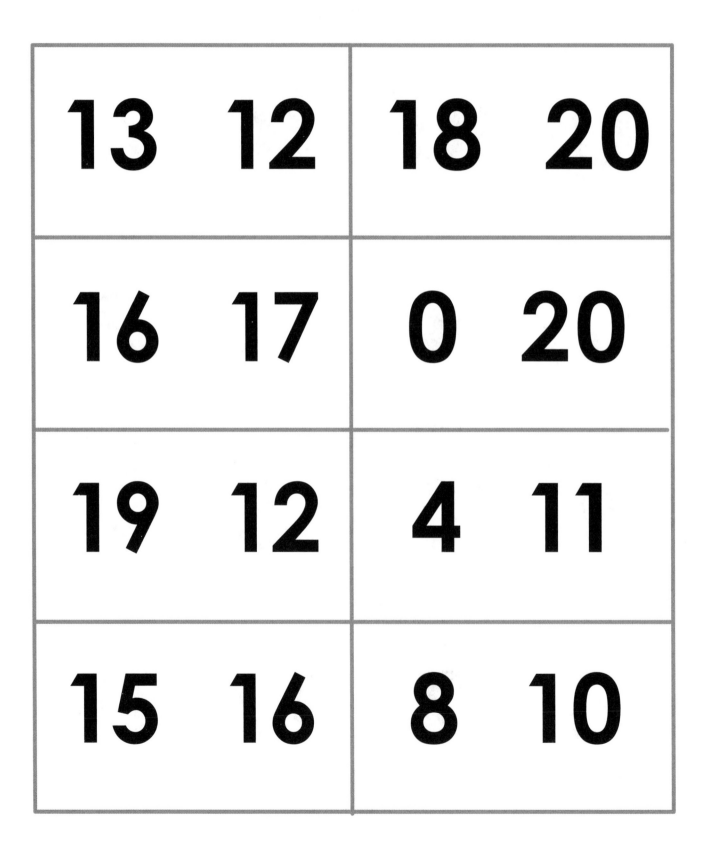

13 12	18 20
16 17	0 20
19 12	4 11
15 16	8 10

Joseph Counts More

Joseph helped Egypt find food. Look at the jars he found. Color the jars with a number more than 5.

Noah Sees the Clouds

When it rained for 40 days, Noah saw more than 8 clouds!
Color the clouds with a number more than 8.

Adam Loves God's Gifts

Adam had all he needed in the Garden of Eden. Color the apples with a number less than 12 in them.

Left or Right?

Look at the arrows in the first box. One is on the left.
One is on the right. Now follow the directions.

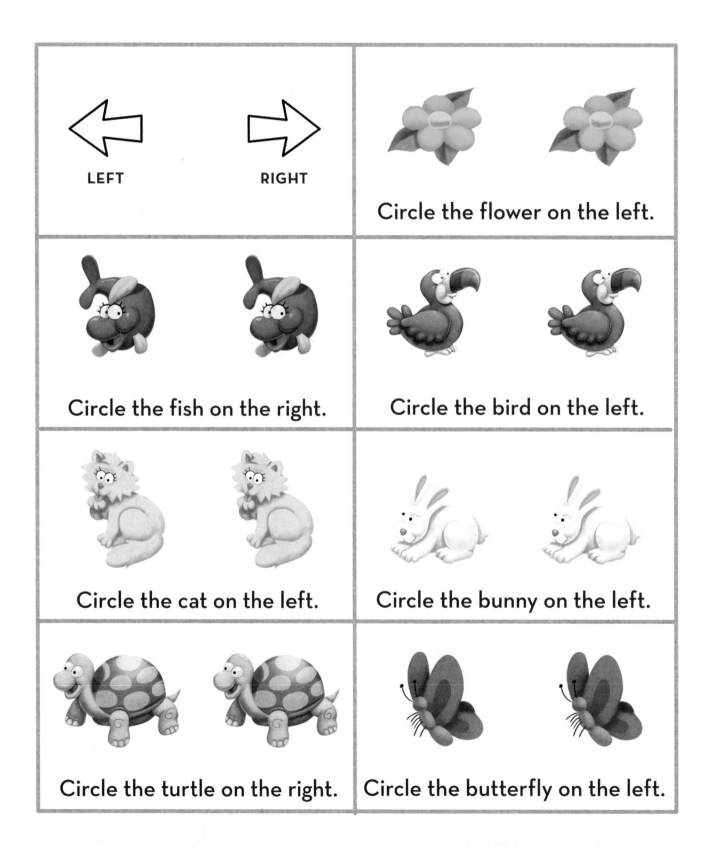

LEFT

RIGHT

Circle the flower on the left.

Circle the fish on the right.

Circle the bird on the left.

Circle the cat on the left.

Circle the bunny on the left.

Circle the turtle on the right.

Circle the butterfly on the left.

Which Way?

Look at the arrows in the first box. One is on the left. One is on the right. Now follow the directions.

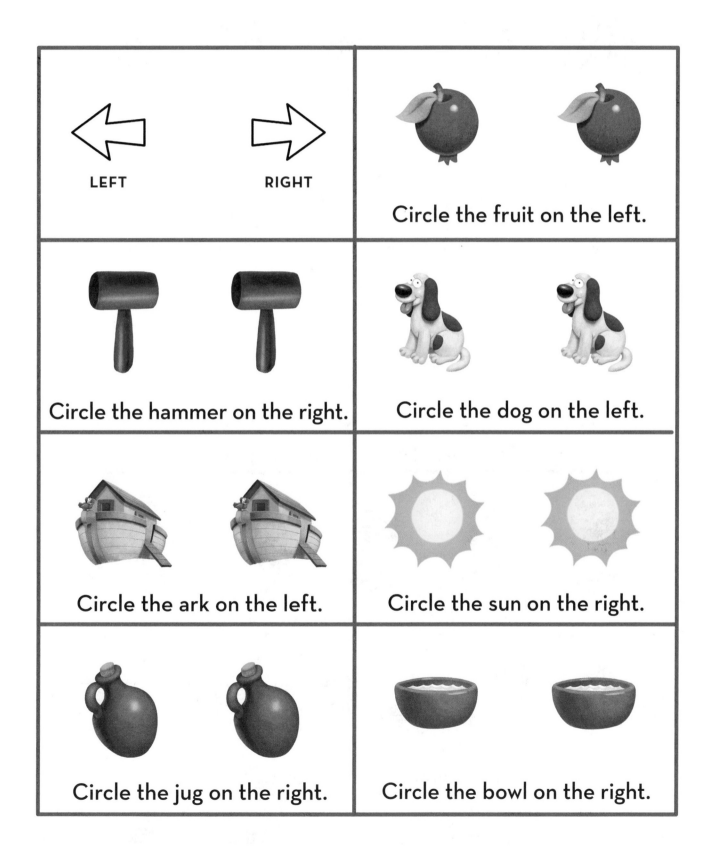

LEFT   RIGHT

Circle the fruit on the left.

Circle the hammer on the right.

Circle the dog on the left.

Circle the ark on the left.

Circle the sun on the right.

Circle the jug on the right.

Circle the bowl on the right.

⇐ Facing Left or Right? ⇒

The Lord loves everything—to his left and his right.

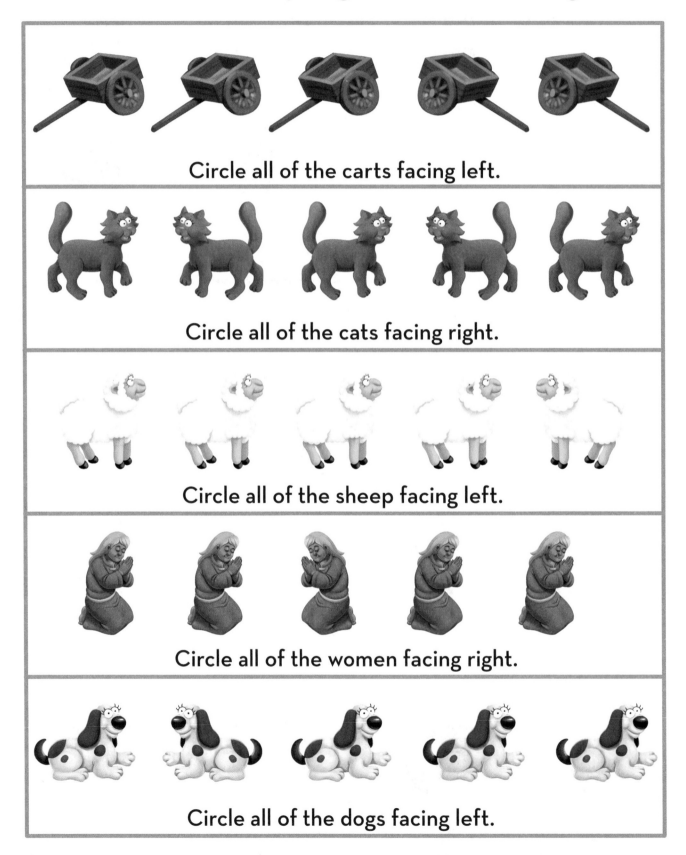

Circle all of the carts facing left.

Circle all of the cats facing right.

Circle all of the sheep facing left.

Circle all of the women facing right.

Circle all of the dogs facing left.

The Lord looks to his left and his right. He loves it all.

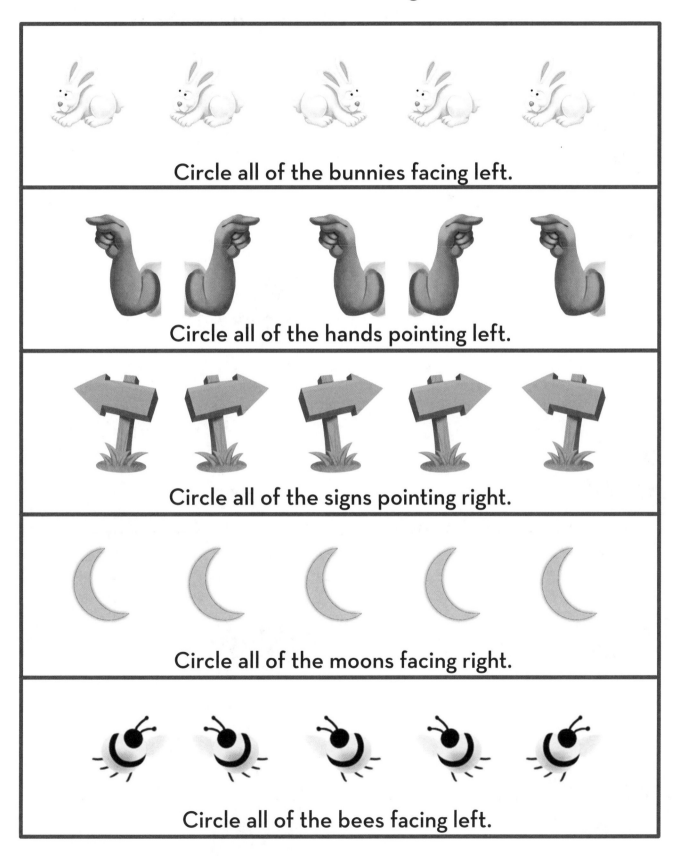

Circle all of the bunnies facing left.

Circle all of the hands pointing left.

Circle all of the signs pointing right.

Circle all of the moons facing right.

Circle all of the bees facing left.

Turtle Ten Frames

Read the number on the turtle. Color the ten frame to match. The first one is done for you.

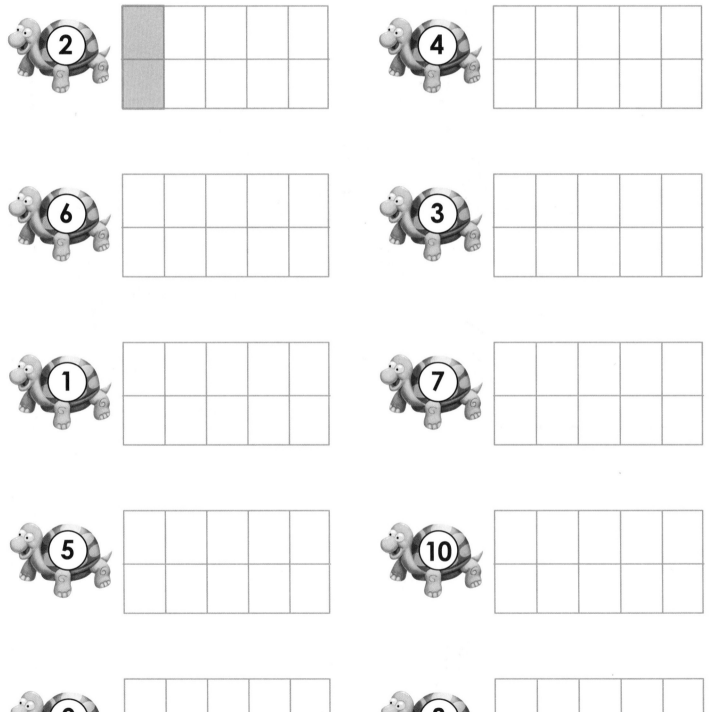

Sunny Ten Frames

Read the number on the sun. Color the ten frame
to match. The first one is done for you.

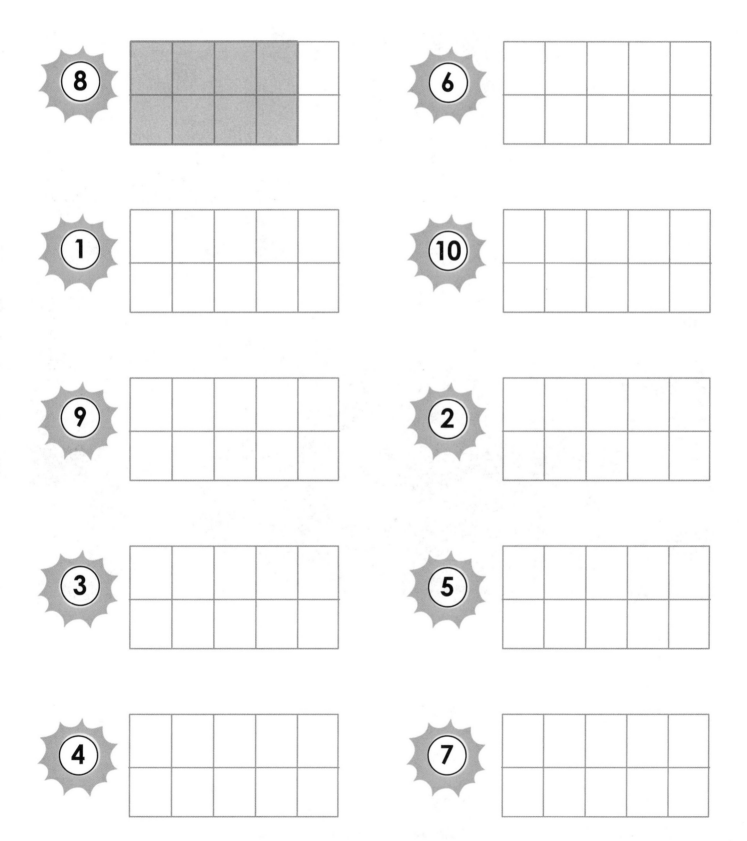

God Made It All Good

God made everything. It is good! Look at the picture.
Count how many:

apples_____   trees_____   stars_____

clouds_____   suns_____   moons_____

God Gives What We Need

God gave the Israelites manna to eat in
the desert. Look at the picture.
Count how many:

manna_____   eyes_____   feet_____

heads_____   baskets_____   arms _____

Number Trace 1-10

Number Tracing 1-10

Number Trace 11-20

Number Tracing 11-20

Where Is My Ark?

Help Noah find the ark!

You need:

- One die—cut and fold one die from page 189 or 191 or use your own die
- A game piece for each player like coins or dry beans

How to play:

1.   Line up the game pieces at Start, by Noah.

2.   The youngest player rolls the die and moves their piece that many spaces on the game board. If the piece lands on a red square, it can move one more space. If it lands on a yellow space, it must back up one space. If it lands on a white space, it stays.

3.   The second player rolls, and on it goes until someone gets to the ark. Players must roll the exact number to land on it.

4.   The first player to get to the ark wins.

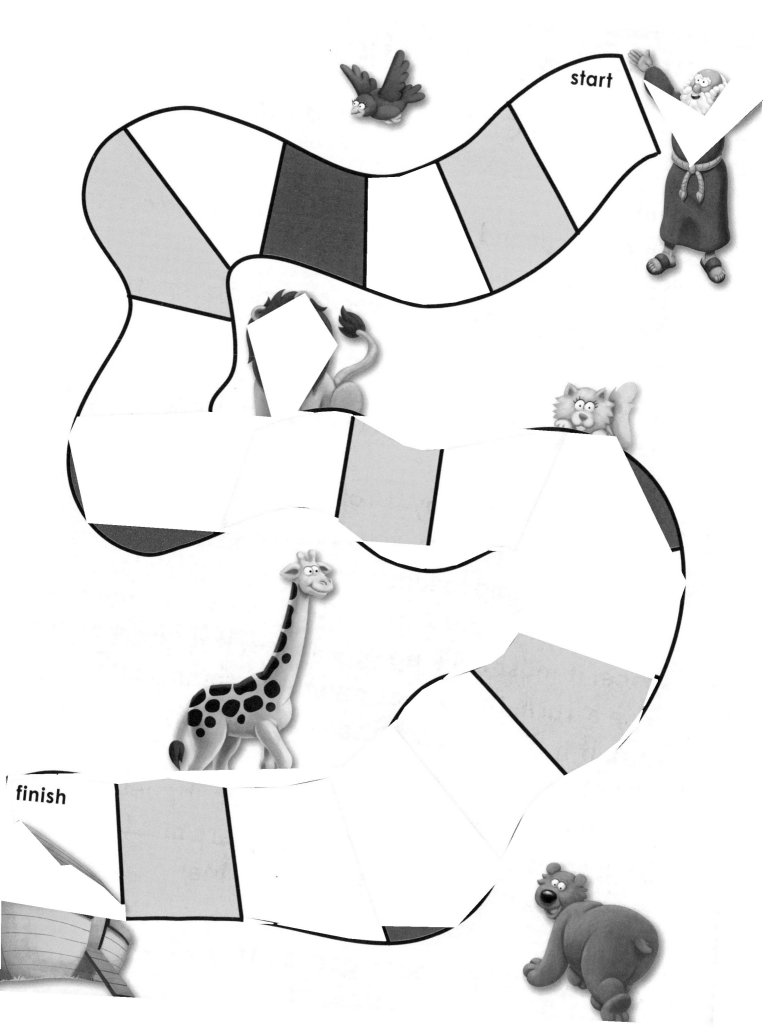

start

finish

The Angel Talks to Mary

Help God's angel find Mary.

You need:

- One die—cut and fold one die from page 189 or 191 or use your own die
- A game piece for each player like coins or dry beans

How to play:

1. Line up the game pieces at Start, by the angel.

2. The youngest player rolls the die and moves their piece that many spaces on the game board. If the piece lands on a red square, it can move one more space. If it lands on a blue space, it must back up one space. If it lands on Lose a Turn, the player must skip their next turn. If it lands on a white space, it stays.

3. The second player rolls, and on it goes until someone gets to Mary. Players must roll the exact number to land on Mary.

4. The first player to get to Mary wins.

start

lose
a
turn

lose
a
turn

finish

Going Fishing

God helped the men find some fish.

You need:

- One die—cut and fold one die from page 189 or 191 or use your own die
- A game piece for each player like coins or dry beans

How to play:

1.   Line up the game pieces at Start, by the boat.

2.   The youngest player rolls the die and moves their piece that many spaces on the game board. If the piece lands on a red square, it can move one more space. If it lands on a blue space, it must back up one space. If it lands on Lose a Turn, the player must skip their next turn. If it lands on a white space, it stays.

3.   The second player rolls, and on it goes until someone gets to the fishing net. Players must roll the exact number to land on it.

4.   The first player to get to the net wins.

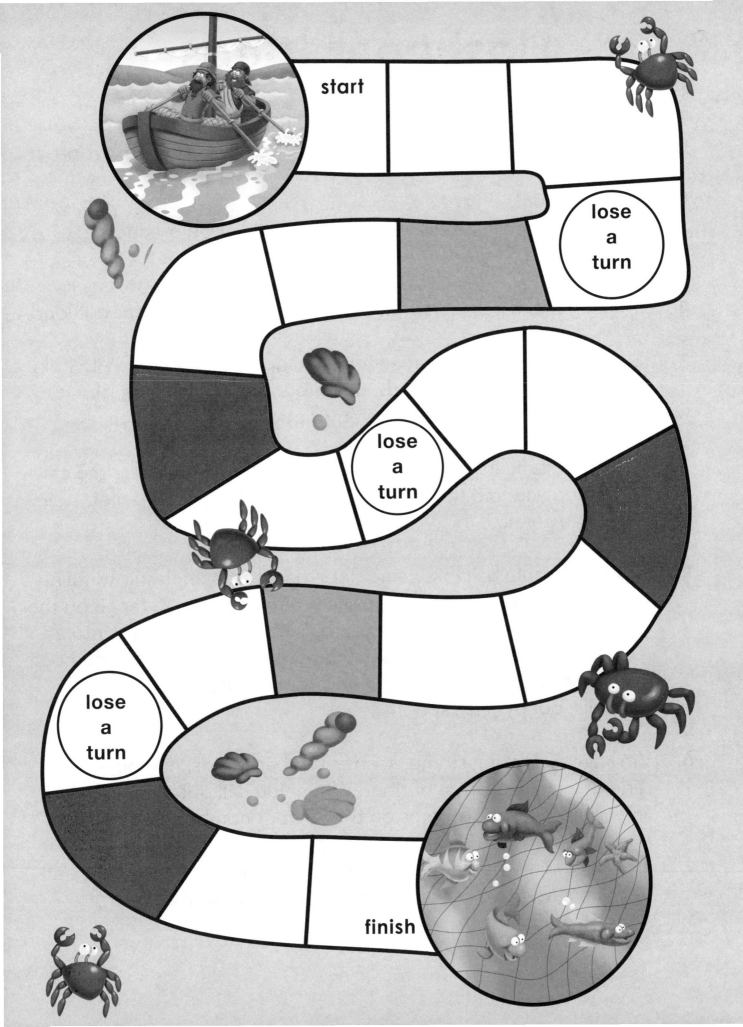

start

lose
a
turn

lose
a
turn

lose
a
turn

finish

Flashcard Ideas

This set of Number Cards can be cut and used to practice number recognition, counting 1–20, and putting items in number order.

More things to do:

1. Say the number and the item on the card as you practice (ex. 1 ark, 2 turtles).

2. Trace over the numbers with a finger and say the number out loud.

3. Shuffle the cards and place them face up on a tabletop. With help if needed, arrange the cards in number order. For more of a challenge, try using just the even or odd-numbered cards.

4. Hide the flashcards around a room or the house. Hunt for the cards and when you find them, place them in order on the tabletop or floor and count.

5. Set up a simple ball toss game. Tape flashcards to plastic containers like food storage containers or ice cream buckets. Arrange on the floor or across a tabletop. Toss a ball (or small bean bag) into a container. When it goes in, say the number, count to that number from one, and then find that many items in the house (pencils, bobby pins, spoons, etc.).

6. Arrange a stocking stomp: scatter the flashcards, number side up, in a large area of floor. When you call out a number, everyone runs and stomps on the correct number card.

7. Look through *The Beginner's Bible* and count other examples of 1–20 images, or go beyond 20 and find 21 flowers, 22 trees, 23 jugs, and so on.

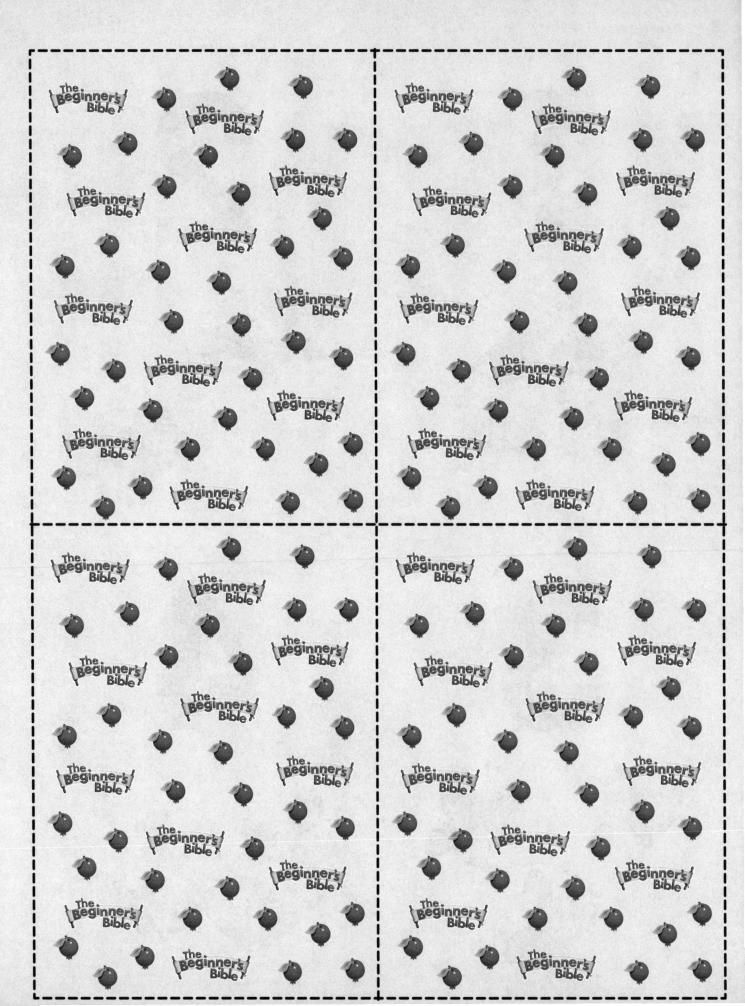

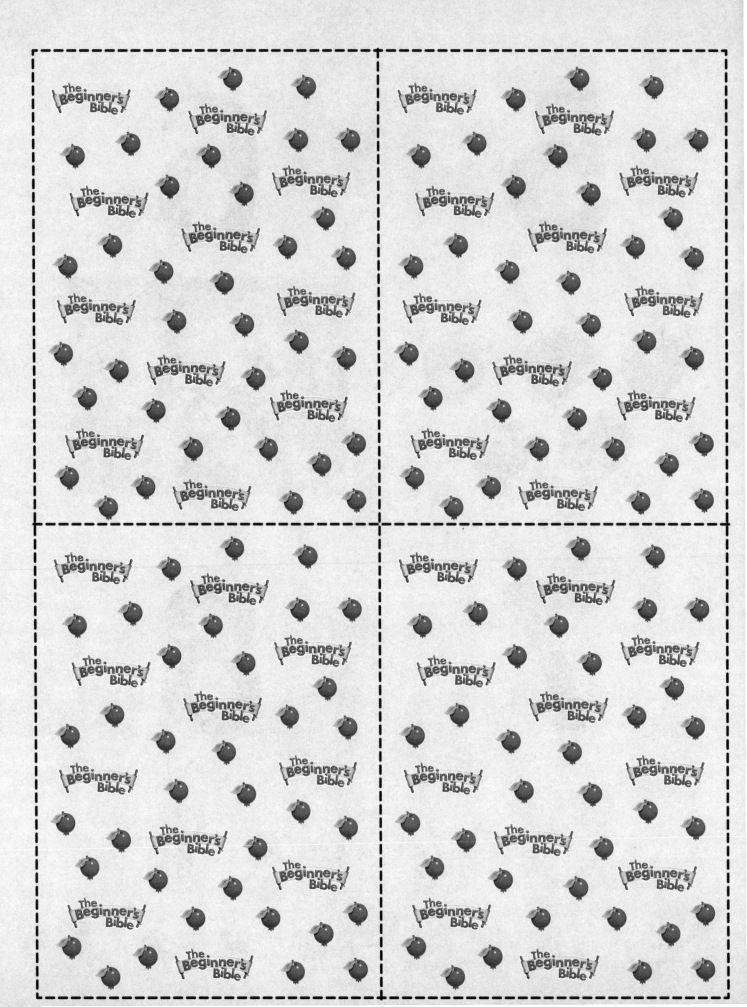

9

10

11

12

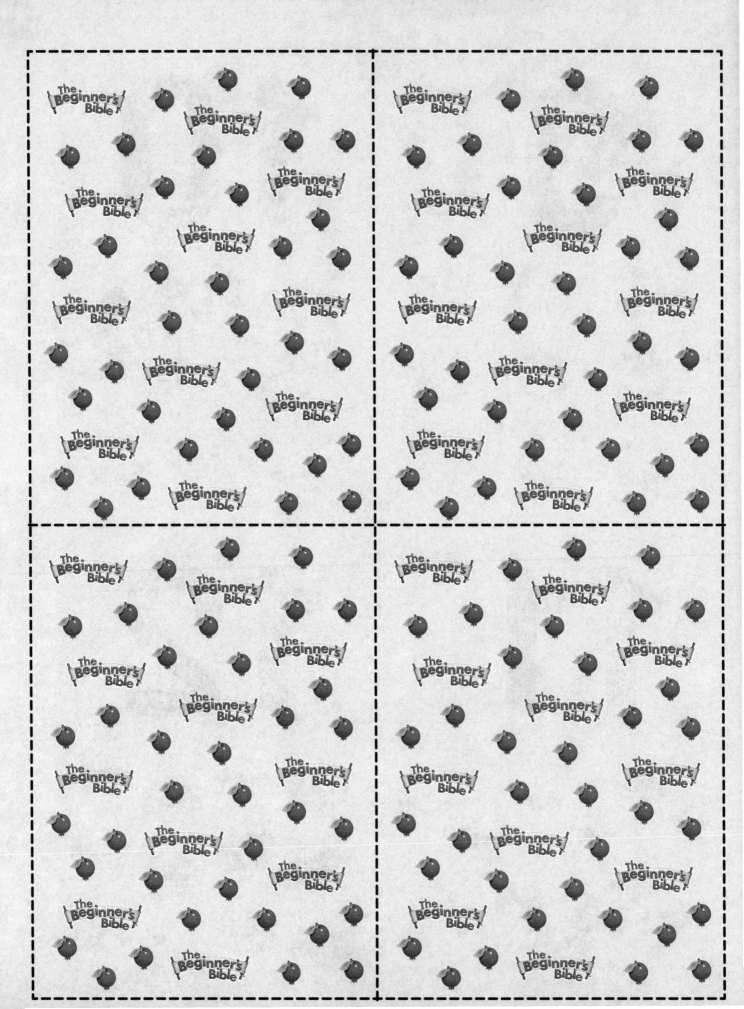

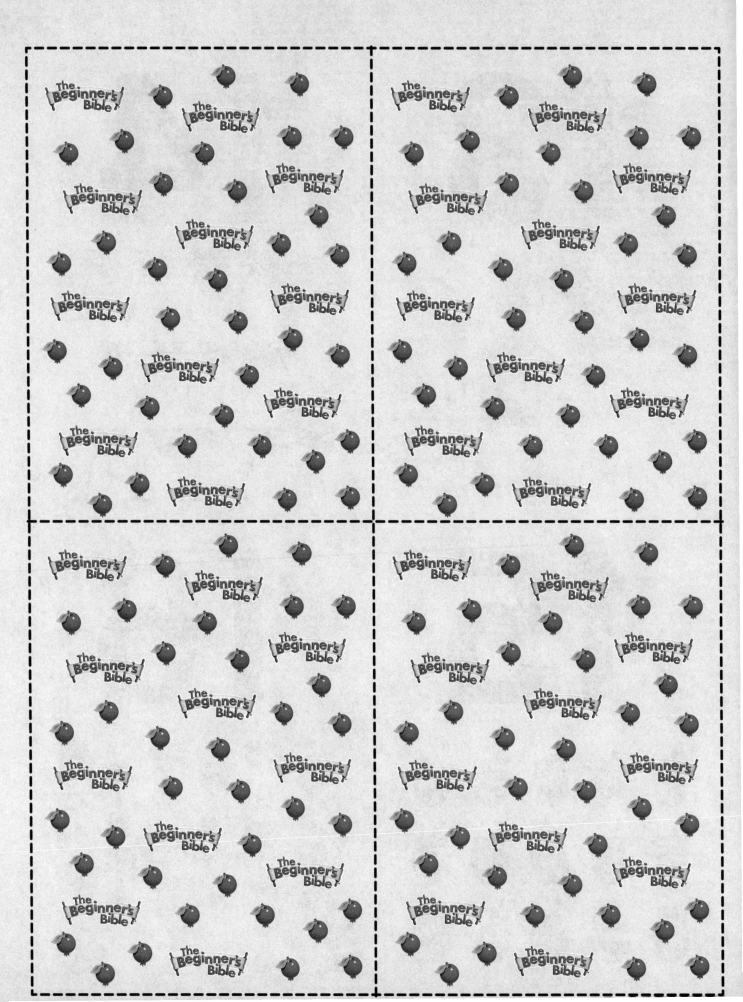

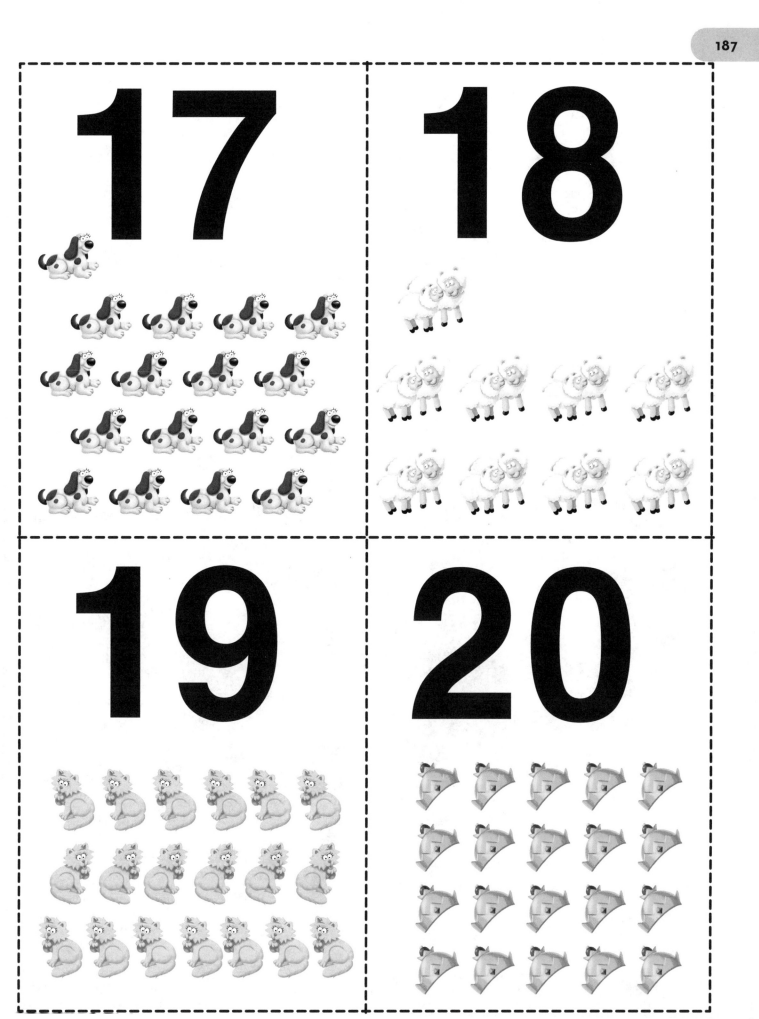

GAME DIE—Cut along the solid lines, then fold on the dotted lines. Tape into a cube.

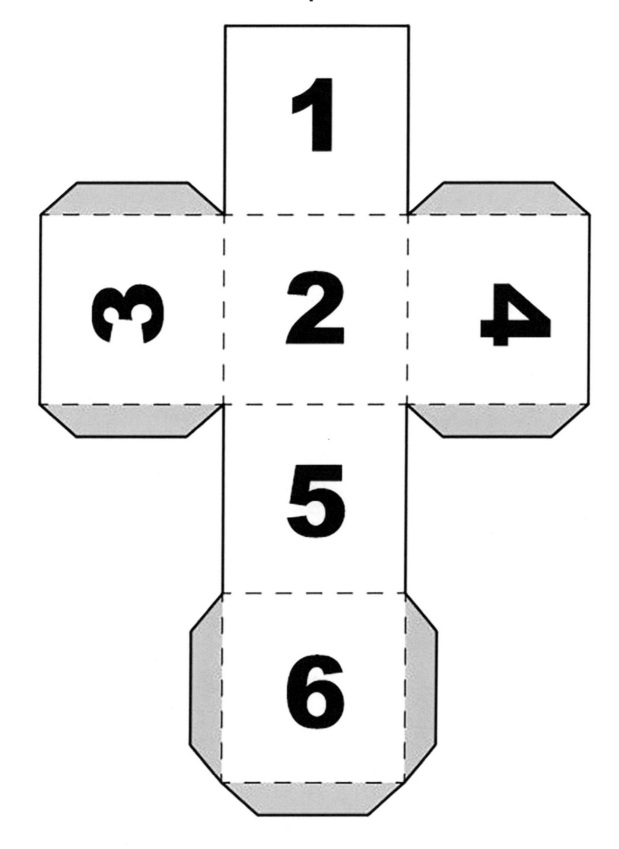

GAME DIE—Cut along the solid lines, then fold on the dotted lines. Tape into a cube.

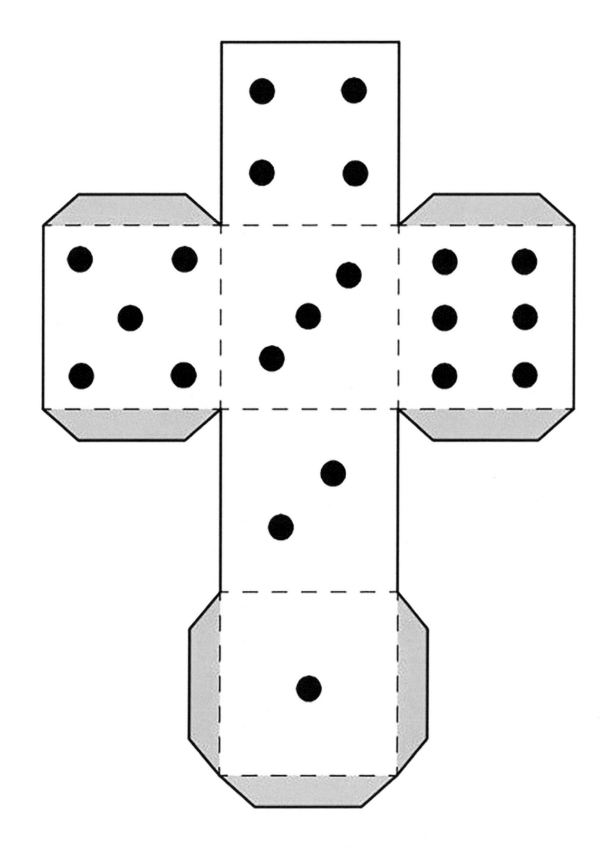